WHEN I STARE AT THE MOON

AT THE MOON

...AND OTHER POEMS

An Anthology by BUDD HANSEN

VEHICLEDIGEST PUBLISHING, LLC | PORTLAND, OREGON, USA
COPYRIGHT © 2025 | BY BUDD 'TK' HANSEN
ALL RIGHTS RESERVED.

WWW.BUDDHANSEN.COM
WWW.VEHICLEDIGEST.NET

WHEN I STARE AT THE MOON
...and other poems

PAPERBACK ISBN: 978-1-7332172-9-3
PAPERBACK ASIN: 1733217290

COVER PHOTOGRAPHY: SUPREME OPTICS PHOTOGRAPHY
COVER DESIGN EDITS: TERRELL J.P.K.
EDITED: TERRELL J.P.K.

WRITEME@BUDDHANSEN.COM

Table of Reads

WHEN I STARE AT THE MOON (PART 1)

The Day Before Yesterday

Once upon a hot summer morning, I woke up sweating, panting, and trying to catch my breath like I had done sit-ups and jumping jacks all night. Later that day, when I got out of bed, I couldn't control it—my mind—a tool I've used since childhood that provided mindful movies and voices of reason. I couldn't get a grip on the pictures in my head, the voices through my ears, and the emotions infiltrating my stomach.

This was during the summer term of 2009 when I lived alone in a one-bedroom apartment in Eugene, Oregon. There was no one I trusted enough to call, so with a heavy chest and a coiling brain, I curled into a fetal position for hours, shedding tears that soaked heavily through the carpet and seeped deeper into the concrete floor beneath.

I rubbed the dampened carpet as tears waterfalled out of my eyes. I didn't have AC, so it was muggy enough for my tears to evaporate onto my apartment windows. But the steam was dreadful. My body was withered. And my mind was spiraling with vivid thoughts and images rotating through my awareness.

After a while, the carpet expanded and exposed the wet padding underneath, where the concrete began protruding my tear-soaked carpet. I stood up in fear, watching the concrete rise as it formed into a rock-solid wall that grew higher and higher, spreading to where it pressed against my chest, making it harder to breathe again. I had no choice but to look away and pace around my living room to keep the wall from inching closer against my heels.

I decided to grab a pair of Adidas running shoes gifted to me while working at their performance center in Las Vegas in 2007. Then I pulled on a pair of raggedy socks and old Adidas basketball shorts. I had muscles to show off, so I put on a faded black tank top, tightened my sneakers, and walked out of my apartment for a deep breath before running up 13th Avenue until reaching the Lane County History Museum.

While pausing my mp3 player, I recall thinking this would be the longest I've run since catching my first runner's high on the Jefferson High School track in middle school. So, I reminded myself I had to run back down 13th in this hot, humid weather. But as I've seen the Olympians do, I stretched my cramped calves. Rubbed my hamstrings loose. And then noticed how one crevice of the sidewalk sank deeper and deeper.

One of the gaps between the sidewalk squares separated like someone was cutting slices of an ice cream birthday cake. Then, the crevice bulged as if tree roots were growing drastically out of the concrete. So, I took a step back. I looked around in case anyone else was watching. And when I peeked down into the crevasse, a jagged, glowing surface began rising from beneath…

(Continued on page 71)

¥

"ONWARD REJOICING, I TREAD LIFE'S WAY;"
UP THIS HILLTOP, A NARROW SIDEWALK,
BUT I RUN AND DREAM AWAY.
"HIGHER I'M CLIMBING EACH PASSING DAY;"
DO SOMETHING YOU KNOW CAN INSPIRE OTHERS,
BUT KILL YOU SOMEDAY.
"HILLTOPS OF GLORY NOW RISE IN VIEW;"
ONCE I'M TO THE TOP, I'LL FORGET IT WAS YOU.
"WHERE ALL SHALL BE MADE NEW;"
...SO, WHAT ABOUT THE FAILING FEW...?

Writings From A Runner's High (Part 1)
December 4th, 2018

On a cold Hilltop of Glory down the street from my home, I run it to secure a story upon my father's supposed throne. Creatively running and speaking to his supposed stone, the top is where I dance, fight, and alone, as he once proposed.

Since I can't speak with him about this journey that I embark on so boldly, during my excruciating runs, we talk until his message is complete and onto a new understanding I approach.

Before his creative *BEAST* learned to speak, runs up a hilltop were as shameful as planes without wings... Flying wasn't his thing, and dying was something he knew we'd all be doing. And upon his transition, he took flight and was carried by the wings of Mt. Zion's calling.

It hurts upon the descent to the top because it's where we die and renew the runner's high of thought. Upon my dad's final approach to Mt. Zion's viewing porch, he said, "I'm here, and that world down there you must never touch—but water it til' the love we've spread is showered in dust..."

7

I shouldn't tell you what that means because I promised him I'd show readers what it feels like to be writing a dream. And be forever in flight with a *BEAST* unseen—who soars higher than eagles, disconnecting with people as love is its fuel—pristine and mistakenly cruel...

¥

Writings From A Runner's High (Part 2)
December 4th, 2018

Dear Dad,

*We both made it up to a new Mt. Zion, my home down
below your throne, and blue like we once grew together and
known. We are Mt. Dekum, alas, where you'll rest well
forever in contrast. Meanwhile, my runs in the city down
here are magnificent over the bridges at night, canvased by
beautiful dark city skies that shine so bright. I recently
moved in with Rocky to work out the worries. He got me
boxing, just like you, but I'm mostly fighting chaotic
creativity...#Amwriting daily despite the past year in
aviation being paid so nicely. And remember me watching
Doug at night? Well, my journal's divine; they'll read it
upon my final Mt. Zion flight...But first, Brazil, Europe,
Africa, Asia, and back to the Nordic. I'm sure in-flight,
we'll speak over the drink I order. Did you talk with my
grandma' Joe yet? She never thought I could become a pilot.
And don't worry, I'm not, yet...But I still reminisce about
riding to the airport from her apartment...I told the
people this would be the last time I'd tell this story because
I had to get the ending from you while listening to Teddy
Pendergrass up hilltops with views...running fast at the end
through a field of grass, I felt renewed, like the December
night I remember leaving you. By the way, what about
Grandma' Dear? Did you ask her about that pre-maternal
fear? I was recently told about how you were never supposed
to be here. But you arrived, proving fear puts the eagle in
joyous tears...Maybe my muse can push others like her away
from their sheer? As long as I don't break the rules of Zion',
sounding weird. And hopefully, no one mistakes my tears*

for weakness. Did you know it's the water flowing down Mt. Dekum's bliss? At least readers will see what happens when a vehicle is over-fueled...Because these tears prove we're rich—our memories are jewels...

—*Love, your main man,*

¥

DECEMBER 31ST, 2018, I RAN UP COUNCIL CREST TO PUT LAST YEAR'S WORRY TO REST; UP AN OLD AMUSEMENT PARK WHERE PORTLAND, OREGON, WAS HOME TO THE "DREAMLAND OF THE NORTHWEST." FREEZING IN MY NIKE GEAR, YET WARM AND LIGHTLY DRESSED, I RAN IN THE WORST TRAIL RUNNING SHOES, BUT THEY GOT ME UP TO SEE OUR AMAZING PORTLAND VIEWS…

COUNCIL CREST WAS "PORTLAND'S ROOFTOP GARDEN ON THE MOUNTAINTOP." IT WAS AN UNPROVEN BELIEF THAT THE PARK SITE HAD BEEN A TRADITIONAL COUNCIL GROUND FOR NATIVE AMERICAN INDIANS; THEREFORE, THE NAME "COUNCIL CREST."

The Animal Which Speak
January 2nd, 2019

These stories, although told on runs up a Hilltop of
Glory, the reason—
An inspiring and thoughtful journey.
In the glory of one story, so cold I had a worry.
My fingers frozen, feeling untouchable like a starlit,
Then ran numb with my body all stiff.

.

.

From the bottom, I envisioned Council Crest,
Knowing I had a treacherous uphill run,
With ease, yes, I stretched…
From Terwilliger BLVD,
I ran four miles up a rocky trail,
Ignorant of the eventual elevation nausea from hell.

.

.

Jumping over mud puddles,
…twas' an animal avoiding territorial gator.
But who art thou in the wild?
Where you don't have the following,
watching you smile.
ZERO eyes on you for a while.
Can you run hard without that, alone in the wild?

For the people I crossed on the narrow trail's path—
...artifacts, as I just needed to slip on past,
Because I'm running until the Council rests,
Where they'll think I've done this before—
As my body's at ease, and sword on my chest.

.
.

Avoiding rocky and slippery terrain, thrice causing my
foot to twist, and twice nearly sprained...
But who art thou face in the wild?
Wet, cold, and no one to carry you,
Assuming you pass out for a while...

.
.

Once in pain due to my calves and thighs cramping,
It was like I'd been here before,
In a tropical jungle, running to a safe shore.
Face covered, only looking up the hill,
But for vanity's sake, my face ain't the fate.
For all I knew,
People witnessed an animal in its space.

.
.

Running under trees, muddy leaves, narrow paths, and
million-dollar homes in between views of trees.
Unlike the ones I'm on this run with,
Elevation couldn't distill this...
I've never even trained to run up trail-hills,
So, I smoked a number to ensure the bliss.

.
.

Very dangerous,
But that's him in the wild,
Very courageous.

But for the *BEAST* within,
He needs a daily training kick…
He'll make it despite,
Running up rocky trails ever being on his bucket list.

.

And about this wordplay thing, I get carried away
listening to rap music and R&B Queens.
I often switch it up, listening to ambient violinists, film
scores, and Rasta' tings.

.

In 2018, I coined *me* a poet.
In 2017, I never would've known it.
First, I thought it, then wrote it,
and soon spoke it while getting fit.
I dunno, I just show up,
And it speaks like a preacher shouting, "Grow up…"
Never ending until he sees the people getting sick of
applauding his trust.

.

Anyways, who art thou in the wild?
An animal tamed and running upright style?
Writes without pop, or style?
Just words of truth for a simple smile?
What's rest in the wyld?
On an exhausting uphill run
and downhill with half the battle done…

.

I got lost, and an extra three miles is what that cost.
Those trails are confusing,
But losing was not of my choosing.

But the animal kept running,
Ignoring the exhaustion and confusion.
Trouble amongst me—
Tired, lost, and miles from my nice BMW.
A black man's wish.
2018 made me a black man writing this shit.

.
.

It wasn't my plan; I just showed up and began making
words connect again.
But with trouble in the wild, luckily, my iPhone charged
to play Juvenile.
By then, an aching foot and two cramping legs, so I
turned up the dial.

.
.

The people saw me stretching it out and catching a quick
break—a much needed inhaling.
Uber came to mind, damn.
But I ran it off after the people saw me,
As if they were of the other clan, lauding.
"Wait a minute, who are you…?" they command.
…an awkward black, mysterious,
But maybe writing, man?
Telling stories in his head,
While he's an animal running wild, like man?

.
.

…so, who art thou in the wild?
Mine speaks like I'm the child,
telling me, "Keep running, lil' nigga,
They'll think you've been doing this for a while…"
But I run and seek soft terrain for my landing feet;

More importantly, I breathe.
Often no ease to the land, muddy rocks, and almost
slipped down, way into the ridge's drop.
Woulda' been done then…
But in the wild, the animal runs until sheltered in.
And when night falls, the people up yonder will witness
his light running free in the dark,
Like a shooting star,
Yet, standing strong like an untouchable,
Christmas star…

.

.

I couldn't believe I'd made it up and down this far.
Pain and agony, I finished running light but hard.
The people stared at me,
Unsure if to say "hi," to me.
But I was in pain and agony—
An ignorant running negro who speaks creatively.
What an animal inside of me…
Last, it said to me,
"Keep running, lil' nigga;
I am the voice you seek…"

¥

WHEN I STARE AT THE MOON

Brooklyn's Bridge Of Glory
January 25ᵗʰ, 2019

Landing at JFK after my red-eye flight,
I walk through terminal, 'whatcha ma' call it, requesting
a ride between flights.
An hour later my Lyft drops me off near John V.
Lindsay East River Park,
Where I stretch before trotting beneath the
Williamsburg to start.

.

Next, I'm on Brooklyn's Bridge,
Running and rapping a *Nas* song to People as if
Brooklyn's where I live…
But no, I'm from Portland, Oregon—blazing to sing
through songs I'm implorin', and,
Impersonating a writer from a body of Zen I run in.

.

First I chant—preparing to voyage alone and spread the
bliss I seek every morning.
Rise and Shine; find me east-coast time.
From my old concrete floor, grew the flower you see in
me blooming more and more.
Once curdled in the dark,
Wishing for a New York City-type spark,
Begging for a vacation; life back then was dark.
Whatever that means…

.

But the silence of one lamb, was silent for my sham.
Excuse me, but I meant shame.
I had to rhyme or else this poem reads lame.

So, I spark my imaginary cigar of fame...
It's my Frank Sinatra-type *swang*,
Projecting dreams across NYC's finest for gains.
I'm on this bridge during a layover,
Envisioning my descent over D.C., ya' heard?
And soon to be 'wheels down' at Reagan, I yearn.
Fresh off a Jet Blue bird, Lyfted to run NYC, turnt',
And no photos taken on this run I earned.

.
.

But that's my traditional traveling way.
Playing on the FDR Parkway between planes—
And on a Tuesday...
Why do I do it?
Because I can write about it.
Use words as my portrait like this.
And mark each verb as the street artist's sketch.
Wait until the next time I rap on that bridge...
There'll be plenty of photos of me,
And not one of them,
Will be taken by me,

¥

Leaving New York City Again
March 8th, 2019

My story has brought me to New York City thrice in the last month. The first was just enough for a Brooklyn Bridge run and rhyme. While it was hard enough to run under a cold SUN, I ran the streets as layover fun…

On my next visit, she and I explored Manhattan as tourists before Brasil between planes, so she also felt New York City's bricking chills smacking her face.
Next, we're leaving NYC for southern cities below the equator. Nose to the south, en route to Porto Seguro. That's far as fuck—no doubt.

We attend a wedding, get hot, dance and sing. Of course, we're day partying, drinking too much like Zay and I did in Vegas '09 off the nasty Lemon Bacardi.

Returning to the States, descending onto JFK's runway and sick from the meat I ate that day, I reminisce about my run. Why? Because…When it's wheels down, it goes down. Thinking about how and why I ran a city and didn't snap pictures for Instagram, I only got words for a rhyming rule, as if people would care to read my traveling tool.

But I'll be back in NYC plenty. To explore more of my singing on empty. Although NYC isn't my city, it's where flights have put me. Neither is singing my thing, it's how I get energy when I feel my legs ain't with me.

¥

WHEN I STARE AT THE MOON

#AMWriting On The Run Between Our Moon And Sun
March 26th, 2019

There was a beacon for this run;
Feels like home, so, damn it, I run.
This is uphill battles for fun,
Where our MOON knows best;
Shouting, "Put him to the test,"
…and run the AM fog,
Prove him apart from the rest.

.

.

And so, I howl with the MOON,
Releasing my stress.
…crazy to believe my dream was to be running,
To write and confess—
#AMWritingFiction from Poetland;
Started at Tom McCall with this jogging,
and marketing mess.
It's an annoying story; I must abreast.
Yet, watching from Dekum's nest,

.

.

He is like me,
Writing cocky,
And so purposefully.
So, what if we are the poetic justice you envy?

.

.

Putting 1,000 plus words to any picture,
Poetry's the plus.
Most only get to the picture.
I once road the bus…

.

.

These words are more than concrete art.
Stop and snap a picture of each word I dart.
They're written to connect worlds with love,
Art is not to set us apart.
But to pull us together and,
Breathe as one, strive for better.
Yet we forget because society is the stressor.
How about that pillar?
A book that remindfully amends racism…
Naw, how about never?

.

.

It could be satire, mixed with Sci-fi and political history
to inspire?
Mainly so people can research true history.
I ran a nine-mile route in D.C. to understand my misery
and running trajectory…
Don't believe me?
Seven-thousand words through those streets of D.C.
Training to later howl with the Worm MOON of me;
Shaking off my demons for the Winter MOON to see,

.

.

And then a panic attic,
No—not one of you wished the best for me.
All for the unscorned of writing,
A warrior's oath to whom he dorm fighting,
Through the migraines of,
…still asking to BEAST as I best keep thriving.
This beacon, skilled and horned.
Running for books and believing for yours.

I run to write and ready the dormant.
Book one is when you'll see me go orange, and…

.

.

Don't believe me?
Read this from the beginning,
But do so while running…

¥

WHEN I STARE AT THE MOON

The Writer's Nest
April 6th, 2019

Running hilltops of glory,
as a driving force for his crops,
…he still worries.
A star shines in networks,
Seeing the dark behind allows viewing from EARTH.
Whose star shines with you;
all day hidden behind the acclaimed blue.
Blue during the day,
Grey when the brightest one isn't shining away;
Who are you writing to?
The world; from an inspiring fool.
With words, an unfaithful rule.
Attention unknowing where it scolds,
Hold it for the *things* ruling what's past and told.
The fuck out my way.
Flying up the Rockiest Butte was not an issue.
Could've been the hilltop of glory way back in that story
from May.
Ran it like I am it;
Watching from the nest.
Wait til' I own the rest…
Butte by no dispute.
I refute, if you try the mystics,
Take a bold cry and be molded acute.
White meat til it's alright to eat.
The watcher knows best.

One dead?
Blood bath only seen by those unknown fed.
An oath too, that dies.
The women whom they will, as well see cry.
Writing from the nest to the people;
Forever aspire a hidden lie.

¥

The Train Of Thoughts For Brotherly Love
August 25th, 2019

From the bottom, you can prove a great birth.
Running through your city, love after one step,
I made it look pretty.
But it's my struggle—
…so be it; I'll run past constitutions so empty;
a statue of past times and misery.
Yeah, they were here,
imputing rules for blissful fools,
…as if we'd get here and continue the unfair schools.
That's bullshit.

.

.

By day one, my detector alerted me,
That world is of cruel shit,
Where the best ones fail in front of many,
And the magnificent don't give a shit.

.

.

The pivot after failing plan one;
Unthink to figure out plan two,
And the third becomes a *BEAST* of a nerd,
Creating the new from the view of a bird,
Eyes gawk as the voice within them churns.
Creating an unreal story that you can't converge.

.

.

I'm no poet, yet, but the inspiration in me turns,
Somehow rhyming, so I run to calm my nerves.
I'm no writer, but the words create a story—
Of brotherly love and how pain's the cousin of glory.
Don't believe me?

Just watch as I unthink at this poetry…
Leading me astray as people think so low of me.

.

.

I'll meet you there as Kane wasn't Abel, you see?
When you compare…is how you'll see me so boring.
Watering rocks in faith as life gets blurry.
Heartbreak writer, she's no longer my worry.
Never label me;

.

.

I may not be educated enough to speak so freely.
Hiding behind labels for recognition?
I'll let anxiety be of me.
When to stop is the pot calling the kettle to drop.
Keep judging your brother Budd,
2021 is when book one's dubbed.

.

.

From love—it's the unseeable language,
'In words, we trust.'
Thank you, Philadelphia,
This poem's from a hot Philly run.
You read, I'm pleased.
And with each word I leave,
In peace,
Ka' Peesh,
¥

I Was Running (Part 1)
October 14ᵗʰ, 2019

I'm the type of individual who often questions why they're here. Where? Anywhere... a position of great power, trust, appreciation, or simply, freedom. We all have our definitions of freedom—so let's start with choice.

I believe no matter how hard we contemplate, the final decision would have always been so. Why do we waste time thinking? And maybe I've read a couple philosophies about the ego, id, and super-self, but the truth is, the experience is all in one. Thinking is necessary, and we must consider the many circumstances we may come across. But a gut feeling will likely decide.

And this is my conclusion after a year of writing daily and meditating. But first, I can't forget about my dear journal. And I have a great mentor. I also have a neat home, inside and out, to write a lot.

I'm fit, too...

Last night at 11:11 pm, I was doing my final leg stretches before my run. The feeling of doubt soon got to me—and to ask, "Why am I here?" I could've just gone back in the house to sleep, wake up tomorrow, and apply for more jobs. But as silence reminded me, no one else was out. Just myself, trees, and the fog below my breath.

Most of the way was dark, so I ran on alert, asking why I do this? What's the worst that could happen?

I injure myself mid-run and have to call upon a nearby driver? Or my mom... So, why do I do this? I easily could've gotten clipped, hit, or attacked by a family of opossums.

Cut the run short?

No.

But then R. Kelly's *World's Greatest* came on. Maybe I'll re-write it, thinking…
(…continued)

¥

I Was Running (Part 2)
October 14ᵗʰ, 2019

The world's greatest believer.

The world's greatest achiever.

The world's greatest overcomer.

Because, oh boy, let me tell you about my problems.

I ain't shit.

Chased a dream, and you wouldn't believe what I left.

But I'm here running at 12:30 am… blessed!

Arguably stressed.

No one else in this space is doing it.

But a GOD who has my hand said it best.

"…the way you choose is known, I confess."

No, this isn't a bible verse; it's my will I must test.

That I write through ignorance,

And be at places I request.

Because honestly, I don't know what I'm doing.

But I trust some universal power…

Above or below, watching me howl,

Up at the MOON because it watches me flower.

…and from the concrete streets of Poetland,

I run to the Hunter's MOON for fun,

So I'll be the greatest writer when done,

It's all the wild has shown me,

Go write it,

And run.

¥

WHEN I STARE AT THE MOON

#AmLiving My Beast Life
October 26th, 2019

Ran that…
Wrote this.
His shades gleam,
Behind them, likely staring,
Grinning teeth to bore the moment.
Grateful the rocks beneath don't fall as his feet go,
One after another, without thinking, his body, tempo,
The air from here won't leave us—just trust it—bro.
The next step is like a free throw.
They'll stare, so smile.
You worried?
You're weak.
Wouldn't last…
Not even in a yoga class.
Tired from what in the fuckin' world?
You shouldn't even be here—go back to Word.
Bum, you ain't even worth the car you swerve.
Then he spoke about a plan, influencing him daily.
Writing to people he'd thank in the future so bravely.
All doubt but internal encouragement set him free.
Leaving forms—but informed that made-men are busy.
From an owned land up high, guided by watchers, all who
spy for an angel beneath him… an origin, but only to
relieve him…and so, he'd fly away so brave, as showing up
was the only goal to have overcame.
There be no savior, million-dollar check,
or luck. Just a, what in the fuck…?
What's there, became light,
…into a future to own.
Just walk…
And sit,
So be it.
So lit,
¥

WHEN I STARE AT THE MOON

I Just Run To The Moon
November 14th, 2019

Last night, I ran four hilltops. The seven-mile route originally has two uphill battles, but after the first uphill running south, I saw another to the east. In a split-second decision, I ran it.

Ironically, my shuffled playlist plays "*Hills*" by The Giving MOON ….

I kept running east up the hill until the end of the song. The hill got steep as fuck… I wanted to get to the top, but I knew I'd have three hills to run by then. Although the MOON was bright, and it would've been nice to see it at the top, I had to preserve energy.

After walking back down, I ran again, taking it easy on the way to my next hill. Then I saw this other hill. By the luck of the draw between two cross-walk signals, it was either which way to continue, the flat trail running west until the last hill, or add this one and run north. The walk signal to my right lit up, which meant the hill to run north.

So, I ran it.

After running the third hill, I knew I'd miss the last hill, which continued home. About .5 miles after hill three, I take a left to ensure I get to the final hill of the original seven-mile route. I went a slight downhill, then up north, I ran again.

Toward the top of the fourth and final hill, I almost stopped…. But with a step to a hop from the music in my ears, I sprinted the rest of the way up, spreading my arms, singing to oncoming traffic, and running further away from the runner who nearly gave up.

Although I didn't see the MOON at the top of hill two, hill four saw the MOON run up north. I ran east toward the Beaver MOON in gratitude until returning home—all to recall how I used to get migraines running insane like this.

For the giving mood, which added a hill, thank you to The Giving MOON, who inspired me to chase a new thrill.

¥

Visions Of A Strange Runner
January 23rd, 2020

Sometimes, we're born to be. Our paths will allow us to see. Years of hearing from people whom we should seek. Emotions respond through eternal feelings, confusion, and delusion, but a pattern of abusing.

We have four significant feelings. Each to guide us to a strange place, but in fear, we stay away. When running, the path isn't seen, so it's in good faith.

Following the pleasant feeling, you read my art. Ignoring the unpleasant vibes, words emerge from the dark. Appreciating the calm *being* that I can hum, as does my soul. Expressing the arousal of a runner's high, strangers see me as bold.

Smiling as they stare—straight ahead, I look but not glare. Watcher of my feelings down there. We're both of the unknown. But who sources feelings as the runner and his dog approach?

We, including the K9, were born to breathe. Walk a path en route to strangers we'll greet. Hear them calm, aroused, pleasant, or in fear, speak.

I run like a *BEAST,* so maybe my aura ain't so inviting. Strangers who'd like to be accepted, a mile for you receptive. Those who want to be heroes get a smile through each mile. Teach a *BEAST,* or they go wild…

Joker.

No one's a stranger. But be careful; some folks are *danger*. They want love but confused as hate disguises their ignorance.

It'll take a while to change their preference. Start today by smiling at strangers—maybe that'll make a difference.

¥

Ain't It The Running Man
June 10th, 2021

Summa runna comma, it's twenty-won.

Gotta short fuse; watch what I get done.

Gimme all my money—I ain't short on funds.

But my writing block's over—that shit was fun.

I spoke and I'll repeat: I am his son.

Twenty-won the SUN shines for my runs.

Modern-day hustlin, my money ain't fussin'.

With incomplete words, I should buy full verbs.

But nope.

I publish dope.

Creatively struggled against these ropes.

Writing a *BEAST* who overcame being broke.

Money issues choking at my got-damned throat.

Went forth anyhow—my body's a boat.

Floating through life just to give up?

Competition should hope…

I don't mope. I just go.

Unlike me long ago,

Writing for broke.

Grab a coat.

It's cold,

Bro—

¥

WHEN I STARE AT THE MOON

A Spirit On The Run
August 11ᵗʰ, 2021

Meet the unmarked *BEAST*.

Hidden retreat.

Best kept secret.

His thing is to breathe.

Wreak havoc through streets.

Running like, sheesh.

It's hot out—how bold.

He even did it when cold.

You wouldn't know cuz' he's slow.

But running, he's fast.

Einstein through math.

Everlasting police car,

Cop and a half.

Devin Butler, you spazz.

You wouldn't know he's a star.

GOD hides him like mom's candy bars.

His sirens don't sound.

Gawking—

[prowl],

¥

WHEN I STARE AT THE MOON

A Smile Written For Los Angeles
September 15th, 2021

In the image of…
Running my love,
Smile, I must,
A creative's playground,
L.A. and it's beachy ground,
Ain't it the running man?
Singing?
What a clown.
But he takes tomorrow,
Dips it in sand,
Smoothens it out.
Do what?
Not just anyone can.
Damn,
How that man ran…
GOD'S running man,
Dance.
Swinging his hands.
He's weird.
That's cause' a beach is near.
The SUN is out.
Ain't running for clout.
Left foot, right foot,
Tired?
Breathe.
Hot?
Thank you, L.A.
That was a breeze.

¥

Yesterday, on my flight home from Las Vegas, I opened my photos app and looked back at a few pictures from last week. One that stood out was the feature photo of this post. It was taken just before our final descent onto PDX runway 28 L from Los Angeles. The story behind this poem is about a dream I had two years ago. As I look at this photo, along with *First Light* by Harold Budd and Brian Eno playing through my headphones, I reminisce about that vivid dream, which birthed the poem below.

Creator In Flight
September 24th, 2021

I dreamt I soared above it.
I dream I fly.
My brothers, shall I apologize?
Bullets through a few of you,
My arms grew wings as I flew.
Shameless, I looked down at you.
Jumping fences.
These borders screwed you.
Excuse me,
The mind fucks us.
History is fucked up.
These eyes detour us.
We're one, but who gives a…
Guilt—how else are we built?
Run.
These legs of stilt.
Each is tall for the mind,
A divine machine,
Keep it off the ground—clean.
Think pristine.
They wouldn't assume this of me,
Creating from miles above.

Running for smiles—love.
Wings of purity—doves.
No, the wings you see,
Delta.
The mountain it passes,
Never blew up.
Until now…

¥

ZAMALEK IS THE ISLAND SPLITTING THE NILE RIVER BETWEEN CAIRO AND GIZA. IT'S WHERE I RAN DURING MY TIME THERE. IT'S HIP, URBAN, AND FULL OF PUNKS. ONE KID TRIED ME ON MY RUN. I DIDN'T FLINCH. BUT THE NEXT THING I SEE ARE TWO YOUNGER BOYS WAVING ME DOWN AND CHEERING ME ON. YEAH, THEY CAUGHT THE VIBE AND THREW IT RIGHT BACK. OTHERS, I GUESS, COULDN'T TAKE IT...

Between The Nile
January 23rd, 2022

Running next to the Nile, I had to smile,
At her, because she stares,
And *BEAST* cares.
Running next to the Nile, I had to sing,
To them, because I had a song,
And silence is wrong.
Running next to the Nile, it's filthy,
But beautiful, wasteful,
A hustler's selling note.
Running next to the Nile, she smiled back,
I'm nice at what I do, it's true,
Because I don't get tired.
So leave me alone,
I'm living inspired.
Running next to the Nile, I ignore the ignorant,
Who step in my way—which is risky,
You're either with me, against me,
Or chancing your destiny.
So please don't f*ck with me.
I'm a selfish running asshole,
Dreaming over rivers between Giza and Cairo...

¥

WHEN I STARE AT THE MOON

Relive Santorini
February 7th, 2022

The wind here is trending,
Each tree blown is bending,
Running, it's with me,
I'm swaying,
...so gusty,

.

.

By the salt on my face,
I exerted energies in faith.
Ran an island by fate,
I once dreamt through all day.
It was hard, I'd say,
Subpar—but hey,
I finished, okay?

.

.

May have stopped,
...so my back was popped,
May've walked,
At least I trucked,
Up hills,
Through villages,
And those steps,
I wasn't prepped.
But to finish,
Was a step,
By breath,
Another step,
Like writing,
There's depth

¥

Village Of Sweat
May 2nd, 2022

Stretching to views,
Trotting thru villages,
Beside these narrow roads,
I slide by oncoming vehicles,
& a dance through the market I go.
My runs are hot, sweaty, and daring.
With locals staring, each curious,
But caring—me, I'm delirious,
…and sharing—a journey,
A smile, & each mile,
Running wild,
Singing…
[prowl],
¥

WHEN I STARE AT THE MOON

Gold Face
May 14ᵗʰ, 2022

When I'm running, I am free,
Nothing matters but the 'P',
Poise I run that's all on me,
Taking breaths refreshingly,
When I run, there comes a *BEAST*,
Pacing steps he's sculpting free,
Smiling faces, "Hi, it's me,"
Waving by to not scare sheep,
When I'm running, I think free,
Like each step, words fly by me,
Some I like, most spit like 'P,'
And like gold you'll prime til sleek.
When I'm running, I fly me,
Spread my arms; they stretch like wings,
Boeing Winglets rise by me,
Running gold for currency,
That's my face, don't look at me.
If you do, it's awkward, sheesh,
You'll see…

¥

WHEN I STARE AT THE MOON

Before The Hilltop
December 11ᵗʰ, 2022

Build it, for they will come,

Some singing, most will hum,

Build it, and til' it's done,

See it, your kingdom rise,

Hot, wet, cold, or dry,

Your palace, a prize,

And a queen you'll dine,

From night to night,

Don't be surprised,

Of past lone cries,

Therefore, build it,

And to you, they'll run,

Shield it, for those who'll come,

But first, yield this,

Your right to reign,

A year-ending gain,

Sugary cane,

Let's get it,

For hilltops,

We came,

¥

WHEN I STARE AT THE MOON

Freedom Wings
January 3rd, 2023

When I'm running,
I am free,
Nothing matters,
I just breathe,
Spread my wings,
And I breathe,
Punching free,
Again, I breathe,
Now I write,
So you can read,
That when I run,
Sniff sniff,
And out,
I breathe,
Bye, byeee....

¥

WHEN I STARE AT THE MOON

Pain So Good
April 13th, 2023

Each nostril I pull,
In air til' it's full,
My body, my tool,
Exhaling to cool…
Each breath I approach,
My lungs need a coat,
It's Portland, it's cold,
It's Portland, we chose…
From sidewalks to roads,
I run like I'm owed,
A spot on a float,
A yacht or a boat…
I run, and it strikes,
Acidic… oh my,
Uphills and I burst,
Set pain in a hearse,
I love when it…
Boy, am I cursed…?
I hate when I…
Run me to dirt,
Yet free when I sing,
"Tell 'em it hurts…"

¥

WHEN I STARE AT THE MOON

Got Kansas
April 30th, 2023

Last week in Kansas,

I ran around a lake and,

Got lost, mad and, got-damned it,

It stormed that morning,

So I had to run through mud,

Got my shoes drenched in fudge,

Tried rubbing off on a rock but uhh,

A rock ain't a rug—and,

Kansas doesn't do dry rub…

Tried rinsing off in a creek,

But then water soaked my feet,

Got tired by a tree,

Wiping mud off with a leaf…

Got cold, as you can see,

Soaking in my outer soles,

But I walked in my defeat,

With a bit of Kansas stuck on me,

¥

WHEN I STARE AT THE MOON

Willamette Black
January 28ᵗʰ, 2024

I stumbled upon a canvas of Willamette Black paint last summer when I bought a carbon black BMW 550i M-Sport. Very fast. It's a model I've been eager to get into since I purchased my first BMW in 2014. When I first called the dealership, they confirmed the car was black; however, I got there on one of the hottest sunny days in Portland. The sunshine was beaming off the quarter-panel paint and shining so brightly against the hood that a bit of blue glistened.

It was far from the shade of Dekum's Blue—but a dark blue that almost made me say to myself, "Naw… this ain't it." When they parked it in the shade, I finally saw the black. And then I kept staring, catching its pristine sparkle. I continued to gaze at this new shade of black while my eyes caught a hint of blue. But my brain kept telling me, "No, it's definitely black."

In 2018, while developing the story for my first novel, I'd drive the Black Panther to the Tilikum Crossing to run along the Willamette river. I'd run at the hours of our sun rising through midnight and setting with a morning moon. The same hours when the river turns black and the brisk northwest breeze cuts through the threads of my Nike running pants. I'd often stop to stretch at a viewpoint on a bridge to look over the city and be mesmerized by its morning glow.

Not many photos would come of these moments—but for the ones I took, I look back at them only for my brain to remind me of what's truly behind the eyes of the photographer.

Through the mornings running along the Willamette, I'd also see its dirty turquoise ripples splitting through the most populated valley of Oregon.

A valley of many buttes and hilltops where I ran to the top and meditated until my legs fell off. If you've read me for a long time, you'd know I'm singing at the top of my lungs until I can stop, turn around, and gaze back at the city. And much like my night runs along the Willamette, I'm reluctant to share these moments because a photo doesn't depict what I saw or experienced—it produces what a lens can capture.

When I first started VehicleDigest in April 2013, it was an Instagram account where I posted pictures of cars and sometimes airplanes I liked from the internet. This blog site came a year later, in 2014, when I found myself wanting to look behind the lens of the photos I posted. But I didn't take the pictures. I only posted them.

By that time, Instagram had become the platform for aesthetically pleasing photos. And during sunsets and moonrises, it was like amateur photographer hour near any of the 15 bridges crossing the Willamette through the Portland area. For the pictures I double-tapped, I'd also zoom in to look closer beneath the ends of the bridges— inspecting the hidden corners and pockets that a filter might hide. And then I'd keep scrolling…

I've run the moonlit neighborhoods and east side trails with a tablespoon of grace in my back pocket. Which is enough to get me through the excruciating sprints between multi-dollar houses and campsites that haven't yet gotten their permits approved by the Oregon State Parks. There'd also be a teaspoon of dignity in my front pocket, lightly weighted because considering what a photographer will show but often doesn't, my integrity sits on standby, primed out of a black man's wish.

…you just never know with the people of Portland.

We're a melting pot of pixels obscured by—

I mean, a camera can capture anything, even the blue tint in my car's paint under sunlight. But at night, it's

convincingly black—Willamette Black—the shade of
black that's beautiful, however…

¥

WHEN I STARE AT THE MOON

Skyline
October 26th, 2024

Cold morning runs through the L.A. fog, so I'm
coughing up a lung trotting for miles, and again, I'm
coughing out the smog.

Parading through the neighboring park blocks over a
skyline this muddled, why can't I see the recording
studio? Where's Mulholland Drive? Hollywood, is that
you?

It's best I save this thought for Monica's Pier
Run because the tourists don't move or evade my lane
like they do up yonder.

I run the 7 pm MOONRISE because the last of the dawn-
setters are resting through our hours of the brightest
bulb of midnight.

My breath is the life of my stride, just as so the lights
over uptown. Good run, good city—but what's the
point of an early race if the rest of them don't care?

My best answer is that there comes to be a stage where
greatness is not made—but witnessed…

¥

WHEN I STARE AT THE MOON

Bore The Runner
December 7th, 2024

I run these hilltops,
Thinking through a story,
When I get to the top,
I look back and—
Oh, good glory,
Now what?
This feels,
….boring.
Running and,
Retelling a story,
Waving at drivers and,
The few who adore me.
Some look at me funny,
Especially when singing.
They look at me running,
Except when it's SUNNY.
I guess it's just me, huh?
Out running a dummy…
Reaching these hilltops,
Then write how it's—
…boring,

¥

WHEN I STARE AT THE MOON

WHEN I STARE AT THE MOON (PART 2)
Yesterday

I ran from the bulging concrete in fear, trying to figure out what was happening around me. But then something else hit me…

Was it just that easy? I'm a runner? No one could've said otherwise… I may not have been an Oregon track star, but the drivers passing me by on 13th Avenue would also call a paved road rocky if they fell face flat against the concrete.

.

.

Many MOONS would pass until writing my first suicidal letters in December of 2009. And to pass time, I drowned my sorrows through several weekends of partying and binge drinking—where they'd learn to swim at bay near the drooping gates of my wailing eye ducts. Which was something of a phenomenon, as my darkest winter resurfaced in October 2018 while I was floating in an enclosed sensory deprivation tank.

The poems you read were written over six years, during which I learned to express and unveil my authentic side after nine years behind a mask. I wrote to show you something different. And ran to share the original voice in my head. Otherwise, another voice would've run me into the crazy house. Or walked me off a Butte over the lands of Poetland.

And so, I confess that I hid who I was as if the role I gave you all was worthy of sharing such a convenient story of a worthless nigga who hated himself to sleep every night.

In the nine years—before TheWriter—I became a car blogger and, eventually, a world traveler, running at places

71

where people would think I was a world-class athlete. This brought me to 2018, when I looked back on the phony smiles I gave my friends and family, only to see the writings over my skin, sorrows coating my eyes, and the grieving of my aura.

.

.

After returning to my apartment, the windows were dry, and the concrete wall was gone. But the center of my living room carpet had a massive brown stain the size of a sandbox.

I grabbed a cup for a glass of Oregon's best *tap* and gulped eight ounces in eight seconds. And then it was a glorious, refreshing shower that washed the anxiety out of my pores and the sweat of stress out of my hair. When I turned the shower off and reached for the towel rack, all I felt was the metal bar.

Soaked and dripping wet, I tip-toed out of the bathroom to the hallway closet until I saw, in the corner of my eye, a large rocky figure standing huddled—and hovering over the brown-stained area of my living room carpet…

(Continued on page 165)

¥

Baggage Claim
November 21st, 2018

My middle name initial stands for Joe. Over a decade earlier, they coined, *"MONEY, MONEY, MONEY, MONEY, …MONEY!"* That's from the O'Jays.

But it was Tami Terrell whom I'm named under. Even in '67, it was obvious this was no childhood blunder, that the mountain wasn't high, or tide low enough under.

In '78, Rose Royce fell onto my soundtrack, *wishing upon a star* to reach global baggage claims and back.

I thought it'd be money getting me this far. Yet it was dreams and anxiety following my heart. And while planning and accomplishing, money became less exciting for me.

Money is what people *feel* they need. Those with it easily let it bleed. Because the 'rich' often don't pay much in taxes. The fact is, it's the reason they increase their quarterly transactions.

So, what are my two cents to you? The pot that called my kettle black? Communities before that brought me back? And I'll go as far as the baggage claim to ensure I'm giving back.

Money is what people feel will expedite their dreams. So why do those with it say it's worth less than your aunty's Thanksgiving collard greens?

Easier said than done. Once you're successful, you'll be reiterating these words like I had once done. Greed might never be the secret, but for now, save up and increase it.

What's forever in the W2? Don't get offended, I respect it. I just pray you do it for you.

The almighty dollar, don't ever bother. Once backed by the *quintessential* pieces of gold, silver, and heavy crowned coins as a scholar.

The eagle on our quarter was freedom during college because I was able to freely wash my shirts that were collared...

The eagle soars high, knowing the people's misunderstanding—they work hard and still pay taxes in the outstanding.

Did the dollars make sense to you?

I once prayed for a W2. Today, I pray to never rely on signing another or two. And if so, it would just be for a select genuine few...

Money can create a belief that if we had more of it, we'd have less grief. But I visited several baggage claims this year, and the promise ended in much grief to endure.

Maybe the security is there for you, rewarded by numbers, underestimating what is now self-blunders.

To each baggage claim, and rightfully so, doesn't the first-captain announce which one to pick up from—or no?

That's an airport operations decision fasho'.

For some airlines and aviators, baggage claims follow them fiduciarily on the go.

Money is what people feel makes the world go round'. Yet the people coining that term twist and turn all night long as policies change, and more of us eventually learn.

Money is what people want for daily living, monthly travels, business hustles, and knowledge muscles…

It brings synergy. Against it, we walk upon a rock in exchange for thoughts upon us to unlock.

Shout out to the old days when money couldn't talk.

Am I serious?

No.

Gold too, is a rock.

¥

WHEN I STARE AT THE MOON

Memo To Warrior
November 26th, 2018

To a Warrior once drowned, self petty of worries; and migraines pertaining drunken stories.

A dream, a story, once portrayed in a crooked frame. But after eight hours, he was frustrated and, again, more worry to tame.

You get what you inspect, not what you expect. For the rain falls all the time, yet we'll talk about it as if it were crime.

But the warrior's story is not of the rain, yet a stable aspect of it. A challenge in sight, wet and cold; upon a rock so bold, we *BEAST* run to troll.

Upon these Hilltops of Glory, a prior halt glorifies a story. If you've read my stories, no need to reiterate past worries.

…as if the people feel empty, needing a void to fill despite the world having plenty.

The black space is yours; go fill it, for love is patient, and the void awaits it.

Dust particles, ever heard of those?

I thought I'd be one of those basketball players back when I mentioned this dream in my nighttime prayers.

But it was best that I give up the ball glory.

Later, understanding it was just a one-in-a-million and not the one for me.

Fuck you, Spaulding.

I didn't succeed there, and still, I write a fighter's journey of running up my Hilltops of Glory—revisiting dreams of past writings and worries.

…on the run from what freed my corporate story, forgetting what inspires a dream of worldly exploring.

Follow my dream and read the rest of my blurting. Understanding my *why* and the runs up those Hilltops of Glory.

You'll soon see in the fighting warrior, what lies a significant roaring boy of peace and novelty.

So, for all of you who cannot read me, honesty's my dignity; I come off as intimating, but trust me, I hold a balance of ease.

My story began in black. My light's the contrast I attract.

After years of migraines, which I thought would alter my story, I kept writing so no fool could re-write what was boring.

Anxiety of the mind, and often physically defeated. Migraines of mine, my eyes hated the SUNLIGHT beaming.

I never thought daily vitamins would help me run up hills at such a steady pace, beneath a SUN as its synergy pulls me up like summertime heat waves.

I once thought that would kill me. But I'm good now. My *BEAST* wakes me up, and I breathe me profoundly…

…into the light, and seek our light shining into empty spaces. If you decide to fill it, you're now a breathing spaceship.

Flying in light where dust will glide. Like a *BEAST* so light, or this memo I type.

And from a negro near you, just know that my head's been alright.

¥

MY FATHER, BORN WITH THE SILENT GENERATION, TOLD ME NEVER TO ARGUE WITH A FOOL. AND LATER, JAY-Z REMINDED ME, "PEOPLE FROM A DISTANCE WON'T KNOW WHO'S THE FOOL." THE FOLLOWING WORDS WERE INSPIRED BY AN OLDER GENTLEMAN I MET AT A PEARL DISTRICT BAR IN DOWNTOWN PORTLAND, OREGON. I NOTICED IMMEDIATELY HE WAS EAGER TO CHAT, AND I DON'T DO SMALL TALK, ESPECIALLY WITH DRUNK FOLK. HE WAS OLDER AND RIGHTFULLY ASSUMED ME TO BE YOUNGER. AS I TUNED HIM OUT, HE SAID, "...OH MAN, WHEN YOU GET TO YOUR FIFTIES, IT ALL GOES DOWNHILL FROM THERE, BROTHER!" HERE'S WHAT I THOUGHT ABOUT THAT ON MY WAY HOME.

Fighting For The Generational Fools
January 11th, 2019

As we *all* took in that last breath,

we floated here lighter.

And as we all exhale this next breath,

we sink further to the fire.

...into flames transmitting desires,

It's why we all care.

Unlike these unfollowing generational fools, scared.

You know them...

.

.

Such a thought, deeming them ignorant goofs.

Or a social medium's lab rat spoof.

Like money is a tool,

without language, we'd all be aloof.

Broke and lonely, who are you among your kinfolk?

Or do you hide, delete, and re-filter like weak people?

.

.

They aren't the eyes following you...

The views are your attention,

It's why heads down won't surprise you.

Easy for them, ignorance comforts those men.

You'll never see success the way others see it spent.

Who and what are you fighting? Money?

Don't listen to other generations,

Their 50s are far from your 60s.

Their 70 is no one's 45.

Our 20s, decades from how they'll survive.

A brother told me 35 is when it hits.

And a mother told me a pilot is white boy shit.

Another told me 50 is likely when life gets shifty.

Don't tell me the road is rocky.

Am born a writer's *BEAST*; assume I'm cocky.

.
.

I'ma do this my way.

Those who whine,

They're thoughts in my way.

I don't *apologize* for turning my shoulder on the sunken

black man that day,

Generational negros must see an odd way

to my wicked verb play.

As if they wanna' shoot themselves,

And what about the writings of my pains?

…my old suicidal journal,

Where the emotions sit in vain.

.
.

So, what's it to you besides simple world-play and a

good rhyming rule?

A generational fool who can speak,
Is the generational fool who can teach…
Same with the dummy in him whom he believes.
Like getting to 50 is my intention or dream.
Projecting my dreams like me is him; he wouldn't dare
to dream on a limb.

.
.

He met the untouchable fool—an untouchable negro.
The animal which speaks,
Running to mountain top peaks.
Unthinking time as the ultimate rule.
I should've told him, you're speaking to a generational
culture.
Am not like these unfollowing vultures.
So, I won't dance to your music tonight…
It sounds depressing,
But here's mine,
Hear it like a blessing.
It's off the fires I was earlier expressing.

¥

WHEN I STARE AT THE MOON

Body Of Dreams
March 8th, 2019

Waiting to exhale was a song,

I waited often to end up wrong.

Just go at it; waiting's for vacation addicts.

Just show up; through the journey, you grow up.

Each wound is a lesson, a reminding blessing.

Breathe in success with meaning, next;

Connect back to the beginning.

Who is it that's been dreaming?

The smile eludes the watcher.

The watcher of earthling breathers.

Breather of Reptilian brains; natural cocaine.

The plan's in the eyes of his *main-man*.

Dove harmless—serpent charmer.

Sweat speaks to the land.

Calming life's demands.

Skin of the clan.

Got damned…

¥

WHEN I STARE AT THE MOON

Watch The Everlasting Write
April 7th, 2019

If my reach could preach to the world,
We'd be in the last fighting days of lost girls.
Fought for by failing fathers,
Who knows that their mothers watch.
From above, she too, was a little girl who fought.
When refusing to fight,
We make up shit in fear and fright.
Withholding a *BEAST* to peak.
Ignoring our muse who seeks.
Solutions from an everlasting leap.
But that's not the answer.
See where the last fight got us?
Cancer.
Eating for anxiety's banter.
You're not reading a negro from the ghetto.
Maybe a negro fighting for the ghetto,
Writing to the ghetto,
Running through the ghetto,
Where the real ones say, "hello."
What a fine young fellow.
Little would they know, I'm fresh from this coast.
Best tap into Oregon's H20.
PDX folk only know.
Oregrown, #AMWriting from here.
I am so rare.
Unlikely to be known.
Just watch, don't stare.
I don't care…
¥

WHEN I STARE AT THE MOON

Shut Up And You Will Succeed (Part 1)
April 17th, 2019

I'm not worried about anyone, but, the more I pick up my phone to scroll, there seem to be more than a few.

Exposing an issue is not solving it. You're only exposing information and evolving shit. The world was made for you, by those who know how to control it as very few pursue.

If you've thought to unthink, do you believe you'd just sit there and leaf? You'd likely fall as they do, but with memory, get up like a fighting fool. Because lying is our ultimate, unspoken rule. Like my grandma Joe told Harold, my dad, "Give him the rules of the road, the 'no no's…,'" and onto California, we drove.

That was years ago. What have you done for me lately, Grandma? Which one? You'd think in meditation, I grew a Batman-like glow. When one influencer left to guide me, they asked at church, "Well, do you still believe? Say so beside me!"

Like, yeah, the story of Jesus is great. I understand now that, as an adult, I can better elaborate. I have to be careful of my interpretation. It could be too original, like Jesus himself, crucified for the desire to be a walking aspiration.

Like many who've descended below the blue, they often keep quiet as their works are divine and true. And showing the people who cannot proceed in thought, needing social media's daily exploration to further just rot.

¥

WHEN I STARE AT THE MOON

Shut Up And You Will Succeed (Part 2)
April 17ᵗʰ, 2019

So, shut up, and you will proceed.
Time is the beacon you leave.
Trust me, time is not the proven enemy.
But the thing that creates an event we desire to see.
Thoughts of ignorance, you should let it just pass.
Like swords and bullets—
A ninja breathes, alas.
Pick a *gawd*, like the devil they present from afar.
My boys below the equator, I'm writing to thee.
Respect will suck you in when happy,
But at par, feel free.
The anxiety will build up when you can't shut up.
Let it pass; a sword of negativity.
The Fuck out my way.
#Amwriting through an emotional past,
With many broken ways.
To inspire the fools who fall for groups,
…claiming their ways,
Are worthy but spoofs.
Am not my way.
Dudes are rude,
and for products, we give zero fucks to use.
Your dollar, your GOD.
Have you met mine?
Don't dare disrespect the hidden thought in mind.
…speaking when the reactors show their true kind.
They can't shut up.
This whole world is about 'I'.
Your title, who cares….
I'll tell you why.

WHEN I STARE AT THE MOON

It merits an agreement.
A respect for society's pleasing of shit.
Ensure that title impacts people you tame with grit.
Your subordinates, they're your tribe.
They, too, are recording your ego trips.
The ego is life.
Wrestle with the middle.
You lose the benefit to shut up and enjoy the shit.
It'll speak to you.
Let you know what seeks within you.
The bad feelings along with thought.
Let them pass for a better peace you fought.
They're toxic.
Like the ignorance that speaks in your bra,
Take action on the good things you caught.
Be cognizant of others...
They're why you have thoughts.
I'm done.

¥

The WHY In My Budd
April 13th, 2019

This is Budd's appreciation to his new followers.
My latest and greatest inspirations;
Ascending to the watcher's towers.

.

This ain't start in the ghetto,
But I started well below zero.
A negro ruling from his free flow.
Wordplay, weirdos, assume you know.
Ignorant scrolling fools like me don't grow.
Reframing the auto-correct for a written flow.
That came and gone, though;
Through reading now and again, you'll know,
Childlike glow.

.

Thanks, Aunty Emma,
This little nigga now gloats.
You are heaven's new angel.
Like you, Buddy's eyes still glow.
People are afraid like the King's post.
Thus, they bow to the King in their know.
Still feasting for the fallin' stranger.
And victimize to unfollow from anger.
Thinking ugly is their fellow,

.

But ain't no Budd in my *why*.
Don't ever Buddy me, and I'll tell you why.
My down-syndrome best Budd,
Barber at four, leaving no hair for my black Budd.

I never asked him why.
But you'll read the why in my love.
Might've assumed in a letter it lies..
7,000 words of poetic love, written alive.
He cut out the why in the toy I loved.

.

.

Destruction of possession
An oblivious childhood lesson.
Negro doll, curly like my best friends.
Hate wasn't taught.
But a fresh 90s haircut is what My Buddy doll got.

.

.

Now running a lot.
Being still for the anxiety to stop.
Used to write about my suicide,
but the anxiety attacks popped.
Panic attacks and whatnot.
Nothing to do with mental health.
Oh, wait, I'm referring to preventative health.
Listen to your doctor.
You can end up like Batman with a powerful belt.
One that defeats wealth.
No, not GOD.
Or religions we believe we felt.
But you.

.

.

Readers be like,
Never read about Budd, despite,
Writing his fears & walking into them day and night.
'B' is for *BEAST*.

'U' is for understanding the need to get the fuck out of
my way.
The rest is wordplay.
But know that kids are the only group safe.

.
.

The why ain't a cry.
The why is why the eyes will never lie.
The deep soul it takes to carry the eye into your bliss.
Most match the intense.
But cannot hold the *BEAST'S* cry.
So they look away in response.
The gift's in his sight.
One we see all night.
The stars, the waters,
It's the gift of life.
Can *thee* gift it right?
Thou received it.
A gift you can trust.
Not one you'll put up to dust.

.
.

Emma dealt the gift she felt.
A little black boy.
With eyes as big as her little nephew.
What a toy.
My Buddy and me.
Right for the running *BEAST* under trees.
Thus, a gift that keeps giving.
Where the land is life.
We live to keep breathing.
Some write to keep inspiring.
Another why for Budd's crying.

But don't ponder at Budd's eye.
This is his journey of tries.

.
.

Like in the wyld, I started by being there.
Like the leaves, I fell.
Then, the dirt, I lied.
So, as trees over time, I grew.
Reptilian brain also grew insane.
I gathered food I felt I knew.
With water, I washed with the others who walked how I
knew.
And out of nowhere, I shined like the sky I often looked
up to.
Slept for rest because that's what people do.

.
.

Gifted ways to be happy.
Thus, I share it with you.
An experiment, you foo'.
It's how Buddy here grew.
An extended gift to you.
And why he's capitalizing letters,
It's what special books do,

¥

They Respond Louder To Your Failures
April 30ᵗʰ, 2019

When I quit my six-figure job for this dream, they congratulated me with questions of why. When I told people about my life after suicide, many of them spoke as if that was a life I couldn't confide.

Few actually understood me, and that was ten years ago. Respect my journey. I've got plans for many years to grow, and guess who's yearning?

In 2018, I became a poet. Now I can dream about flying out to Santorini, and to the child in *eye,* I owe it.
My story starts here. Fighting a daily fear. But fear is a choice; like my many failures, perspective is held in the void. You decide. Life is for you to confide. Start whenever you choose and thrive.

I fly best on Tuesdays. I think it's those closest to me who question my life's choosing. But when the voice appreciates, the quiet ones decide to hate. Because failure be their levy. We work hard on Tuesdays, into failure is what I'm aiming.

We fight today what confronts us tomorrow. Some look, thus, forever in sorrow. I'm from Portland, Oregon; we've made it a habit to bust ass and keep trailblazing. I was confused about race. But only in a certain space. Fighting the everlasting write, what's the name? Abundance is in everyone's gain. Just aim to fight for the city you claim.

As failure prompts their speech, we watch. And never react. If you do so—you, too, will succeed. Just watch.

¥

WHEN I STARE AT THE MOON

A Resting BEAST'S Fate
June 27ᵗʰ, 2019

I'm not better than you.
I'm not louder, either.
If I held my breath long enough,
guess what? Me too…
The stars will shine forever; just look up.
I look different because it's what's carved of me.
It was best; otherwise, I'd be depressed.
If it weren't for white people, I wouldn't be here.
If it wasn't for black people, I'd still be in tears.
Who's to blame, and for what?
Overreacting to a what in the f*ck?
I'm not different because I want to be.
Nor do I believe I was born to be.
But the fighter in me,
Reminds me how black is free—
…darker than the darkest under our SUN and tree.
We're a fighting race,
But the black is the surviving stake.
Call me weird; I, too, have a difference for you.
I'm from Portland.
They tell me we're weird.
Try that and be black.
Don't ever give me that crap.
History only reminds us how differences come back.
To no one—I'm saying that…

¥

WHEN I STARE AT THE MOON

Bearing Tears Before Flight
August 18th, 2019

When the buffalo's in love, his horn floats the torn.
Hearts of society spread love in a variety.
Fly swatting the deep, quieting the sheep;
You people don't think.
He sings what he believes,
Thoughts inhaled too deep.
It's how he breathes—and the next move,
even he couldn't relieve.
Your pain and agony to insanity,
His character of no one's bribery.
But a channel inviting the mystic of *thee*.
Divine IX smacking a crime.
Hell naw, we don't cry from gate A-5.
Ten years from now,
Would you still be holding my shrine?
I don't know who hears me; am not crying in fear.
With trust and hope, I don't know where the means
come from to continue and bloat.
I miss my girlfriend, yeah yeah, boo hoo…
But we bore it all for dreams to take off, woo hoo…
You'd miss her too,
Likely go crazy for not sticking next to you.
But a girl's gotta do what's only in a few.
Leave to sustain a better you.
People don't change; they grow to have a better view.
And into the self of admiring virtues.
Here art thou cry,
I'm not hurt away from you.

¥

WHEN I STARE AT THE MOON

Watch Close Enough You Get Smiles Back
October 5th, 2019

What does your deepest desire want with you? Do you question it? Or the feelings of push that either hold you back and suddenly stop you in the moment? You look back to think, "What the hell am I doing?"

Smile and laugh at your spinning thoughts.

Is time so precious that we must respect it to get what we want? Or patience, the understatement?

Sit long enough, and you'll get what's coming to you. Either nothing or whatever your past owes you. Note to self; do not carry the weight of owing; you'll be there forever.

Whether or not you'd like to think of something to do out of boredom, what's coming to be will be. You're nothing but a moment.

Be your own guest and desire what the next moment shall be out of curiosity. Are you curious if someone's watching you? Maybe GOD, or some almighty being who's powering all those breaths we took on this lovely first Saturday of October?

You can get curious enough to come to any conclusion. But if your means is GOD, I've been thanking him in peace. The peace I needed to inspire just one more person.

Not everyone feels that their life is fucked up. However, I'm on Facebook, and people make it clear some of us are stuck in sick, self-destructing patterns.

Do I sound like I'm judging? From my perspective, I may

be. If you knew me well enough, it's not hard to see the patterns I'm stuck in.

Awareness.

What are you aware of that you accomplished today? So, it's Saturday, and if you forgot to smile at someone, then do so after reading this.

Watch yourself.

Like the mirror you practice that smile in, watch it smile back. Do it long enough, and it gets creepy.

Everything else starts smiling back…

¥

So You Won't See What I See Out Of
October 10th, 2019

Two of them, however, stressed.
Blinking to protect them; blessed.
Resetting the friction between lids; caressed.
Bright as day, through them, I can say,
What pleases them in a mindful way,
Maybe the apple of it?
My eye, my mouth.
Now breathe, what all else does.
But some of us dehumanize.
What does that mean?
Uncounted people, your brothers, too.
I've learned to see into things, not of this world.
Simply put, nothing but forms,
And a rock beneath to walk on.
How far am I willing to go,
To connect a world, I feel I must show?
Far enough they'd laugh,
…at a little boy who thinks one moment is worth last
year's cash.
To make everyone happy, having it all,
But some must stall.
Because I, too, have anxiety.
It's in the eye I best keep from ya'll.
Hard to say who I am in society…
I'm fortunate to write words from inside of me.
So now…
Can you tell what my eyes see out of me?

¥

Lions Don't Lie
November 8ᵗʰ, 2019

Create a space so the mood can open.
#AmWriting to people I hope to rope in,
To dreams I once deserved.
It's what I must stand to earn.
We are people who make the future.
We are creatures who remember the past.
Some connecting for an everlasting grasp,
Onto others and our love outlasts,
The pains of whom we may laugh.
Navigate to the top for a victim to be inspired.
…from there, a survivor must be transpired.
But never forget who propelled you aspired.
It's those looking up to say,
"We helped you, so don't give up, okay…?"
Otherwise, they'll deem you expired.
What's worse, a tree on fire?
Or a lion'd up liar?

¥

WHEN I STARE AT THE MOON

The Cry Of A Lone Wolf
December 29th, 2019

First of all, they don't cry. When the tears of joy are shed, it often confuses those watching. They react in ways as if the weight was their burden. Who knows what an average layman would do alone, cold, and food at low rations.

Meanwhile, to a temple, it approaches, the lone wolf that is, might it ask what the others were thinking? In some regard, no. For we've heard the sayings of sheep, and no wolf will hear. However, the temple would need to be sacrificed if securities need restored.

This is the story of the untouchable lone wolf—it has no name and doesn't understand its gender. A story without a beginning and no ending. The interactions between two individual's journeys create the illusion of two stars shining on each other. What exactly do I mean?

A lone wolf only knows its own story. You cross it, you're it; now its glory is you. Judge a man, and you hold a subconscious grudge against that man.

Did he not take the same breath of air you took? In this story, I'll do a much better job at separating the lone wolf from the animal which speak—humans, in other words.

Here's what you'll learn about the lone wolf; what they do alone, how they find their next food source, and proof they don't cry. Or, you could see the process of me learning they do cry because I honestly don't know if they do.

Hell, I just read up on what a lone wolf meant. Welcome to Budd's storytelling world, where I dream of writing movies about a lonely ass wolf.

More on this bullshit write up later…

¥

From The Void, We Regret To Feed
January 5th, 2020

Before a motivating meditation for Monday's matter,
Quadruple M's for readers to chatter.
My aiming vice to dull it.
Seattle won, and now I can cheer.
Whew… the holidays are over, now work from here.
Did you forget life's a blessing through holiday tears?
Fly the serpent's way or sway the moral's prey;
…just don't lie.
Be well as drivers steer, pilots fly, and doctors save.
What's next is the new inviting world of crave.
Finally, owning up to the new you so brave.
Dare to doubt, limit the cries, but love.
For each angel awaits you, in trust.
They guide so fairly, like dust.
Saying, "Slow down…!"
But only if you must.
And never—
"…give up."

¥

WHEN I STARE AT THE MOON

What They Say About Dead Clocks
January 24ᵗʰ, 2020

For today is enough.
But why don't we feel so?
We work hard daily, and weary stunts growth.
We, including I, want too much.
What we have is what we get.
Want more?
Some of that shit you must forget.
Don't work harder, but smarter, they say.
Who in our world is they?
Did they make it past the enoughs of yesterday?
Fulfilling their wishes into a forever today?
They, like we, wanted just as much as *thee*.
Thee, like he, and she, are we.
All pronouns include us *beings*.
Believing tomorrow would be the place of easing.
It'll always be today.
If you're reading this,
There will always be a tomorrow to prey.
You can't prove yesterday was here—
But memories help.
Of a calendar, life chapters, and our illusion of time.
Like Tom Hanks said, the ultimate sin is the ignorance
of time.
We struggle and get over it.
Struggle again and say 'fuck it.'
Continue to struggle, then identify with shit.
We attach.
Like our desires, we attract.
Our struggles with time react.
Nothing's wrong with that.

Work off a dead clock;
At least you get it right twice a day.
But that's what they say.
So, why try being on time,
...if we often get it wrong anyway?
¥

Because There's A Journey Within Lasting Forever
March 8th, 2020

One, two, and three,

He opens to beauty with his *BEAST*.

You'll be standing face front to his home,

But never see the door to his throne.

Four, five, six,

I, too, am often tired,

But through action, the day awaits in bliss.

Feel for the next best thing to do.

It comes at a price and is hard to explain.

Seven, eight, nine,

Mix the days with true spirit and sublime.

I eat either in silence or with peaceful music—

No phone.

In gratitude for, there were days I couldn't eat at all.

Ten, eleven, twelve—

What comes next? Sometimes, nothing,

Welp…

Sing if your soul yearns to shout.

Breathe if your *BEING* drowns in doubt.

Thirteen, fourteen, fifteen,

Tell them what it's like living a divine dream,

…especially in today's culture and society.

For one, I must ignore the outside noise.

They, and it, are the nightmares testing *THE BOY*.

People expect rhythm, but words are all I give em'…

¥

What I've Done With The Forks In My Road
April 28th, 2020

Felt alive by it,
Grabbed it to eat steak with shrimp,
Went forward to spoon my latest pasta dish,
Said fuck it with nothing to lose—am not rich.
But ate well through faith, visualizing a future in bliss.
The next best thing to be grateful for is your breath.
Let go and relieve the illusions of stress.
Don't ever let someone tell you the road is tough.
They're projecting the latest challenges in their fuss,
Or, what it'd be like if they hopped into your rut.
But go ahead, fuck it up, and do what's love,
Do what's trust—accept the rarity of actions in us,
Because not many will guide you.
You only gotta' show up and show out.
Don't listen to scary folks' clout,
The others' doubt.
Be the fork that no one eats about,
Poke the air, eat the rare, and let them stare.
Don't look back or glare,
They'll always be jealous,
Because you made it there,
Fair and square…
Now, go fork those haters.
Just be aware,
You'll eat alone.
So, do you dare?

¥

You Can Read A Goodnight If You Want To
June 15th, 2020

I'm tired.

My day expired.

Soon, dreams to acquire.

If lucky, they'll transpire.

But what's required?

Closed eyes for miles?

Good and bad of my trials,

…and tribulations of a past dire?

But I'm tired.

When will time retire?

When I sleep for miles?

As if time stops for a while…?

Then, return for more trials?

Turn the dial.

Blow it by breath.

So our SUN ignites the rest.

Now I have energy.

Suddenly some synergy.

Something's gotten into me.

It must be these words.

Fueling a tired *being*.

Now, leave me be.

Goodnight in peace.

You, too, shall find a speech.

To guide you into a synergy.

Again, I'm tired, and now I sleep.

I trust you enjoyed a good night's read.

¥

WHEN I STARE AT THE MOON

Smile, That Too Is Contagious...
July 19ᵗʰ, 2020

Ask, and you shall receive.
Mask, or how dare you sneeze.
My gosh, be sanitary if you breathe.
I'm sick of hearing about this virus, LEAVE.
Some scared, a few overdo it,
and leaders, who to believe?
So much for clarity,
And we're seven months into 2020…
The chaos entertains, but it leaves people so empty.
"Ok, we're just joking, guys, let's pull back the curtains,
SURPRISE…"
Or…
"….pull off those masks;
it was a global fire drill gone very, very bad."
I'll stop there; it's not what I want in this ask.
There's also much left to say about that;
And I don't put info out like that,
Moving on to the fun part of the day.
Where these words fly off the screen of a reader's
phone, tablet, iPad, laptop, or office at home.
Where you stay home all day, if you're like me—
alone to *play*.
Like the summers in high school and middle school,
when time moved in a bag of clay.
So much to do with it, more time than we needed,
anything in the fridge, it'd be eatin'.
Before Mom or Dad walked in,
Pretend I was reading.
They say I was a spoiled boy, but I don't see it.
Now that I've said it, maybe you get it?

It has to do with the answer; remember my question?
Yeah, I received it.
Likely curious enough to keep on reading.
Sorry, not sorry.
I like this song, so I'll keep singing…
Hold that thought and enjoy the proceedings.
Beaming on my arm as the SUN keeps shining.
It's easy, like a Sunday evening's dining.
Get up and do something if it's the right timing.
If you do it with a smile,
It'll make this poem inviting…
I'm inspiring you to do something exciting.
CARPE DIEM more than you ever.
Go write yourself a letter.
And don't read it til' forever.
But start with your smile,
And how today it gets better,

¥

Who Are You Alone?
October 17th, 2020

I'm me.
I think…
Sometimes I don't think.
But that's what I think.
I think I'm a walking contradictory.
What do you think?
I don't care…
about what you think.
To be clear, however, you're reading you.
A thinking coup.
You can't read me without thinking of me.
I'm black with a story of struggle.
Negro hair, my shit got a glow, tho'…
I don't care.
I'm a bad, writing man.
I'm not ashamed, bro; that's my jam.
Artists are weird.
Have you seen one behind closed doors?
Yes, only they, will get it.
Some are just not as sick behind closed doors with it.
But that's what I think.
Which doesn't matter, does it?
You can't prove it.
But say it.
Confirm you *thinked* it.
Can't you read it?
It's who I am.
A bad man and rhyming without trends.
So meet *BEAST*.
The loner writing your friend.

¥

WHEN I STARE AT THE MOON

Within A Dummy
July 1st, 2021

Why must we feel so empty sometimes?
Venturing through the void—a state of mind.
Demons lie there too,
Cunning and kind.
Vulnerable to you,
But a secret there lies.
As a place of nothing,
You won't find not one dream,
And the queen there knows everything,
So you must tiptoe or lose something.
You ask, "What's that thing?"
Well, to lose implies a win.
Although there's no 'I' in team,
There sits many 'I's between winning.
Each member must win.
And all 'I's must believe within.
Much like free thought out of the void,
Sought out of an empty vehicle.
Speak lively to succeed tenfold.
Understand we're the words from null.
Or a dummy with a wheel-less brain—and skull.
Be tired or at least a driven bull.
I promise, it's no vibe,
But a choice,
Or die.
Bye…

¥

Some Hurt, So You Don't
August 3rd, 2021

Your anxiety is the prize of me,
It awakens the creator.
Your right to freeze,
And be so meek.
You stress to unrest,
Blow it like you own it.
What's that exactly?
Your soul—it's almighty.
And brightening us lively.
Loving and thriving,
Learning from those conniving.
We correct them,
Then pry them free.
Because they're us.
How surprising…

¥

WHEN I STARE AT THE MOON

Yum Yum, Eat Em' Up!
January 31ˢᵗ, 2022

I'm not above it,
I'm of it.
Cooked fresh, seasoned,
And steaming out of ovens.
Hot pan, watch your hands—
It's best you should glove em',
Set me atop the eye,
Simmer me right.
Scoop me lite,
I'm hot like a pie.
Well-rounded and nice,
Sweet and neat,
…what our belly will fiend,
From chews by our teeth,
Chunky but sweet,
Moisting through heat,
Tendery meat,
Like butter on wheat,
Grainy type seeds,
With eggs by our tea,
Staycation me, please,
It's morning now eat.
So Bon Appetit,
This oven's at ease.
I'm of it, so please,
I'm flyin' to Greece.
Reread to believe.
I'm done here,
Capeesh…
¥

Upon Arrival
February 12ᵗʰ, 2022

Poetically speaking,

Motivated and peaking,

.
.
.

Nomadically inspired,

Am traveling transpired,

By these sleepless nights,

I awaken to excite,

These plane rides like beach kites,

Cuz the air lanes in sight,

…what I soar through to explore you,

Trailblazing unseen routes,

I'll get to you—I promise you,

These inner guides, like Tourguides,

Some hustlers with jitterbugs,

I promise you they're good guys,

Like an island's crazed birth fight,

Its eruption's a birthright.

¥

WHEN I STARE AT THE MOON

Travel P
February 20th, 2022

P ain't for power if you got it.
Pivot, reroute it—
never proceed how you started.
P ain't for protest—
must've seen the reactive unrest.
Copy, don't paste—
reread and regroup;
it's the proper humane pace.
P ain't for panic.
…no entity in this world pushing P for paper.
The P used to page her,
Broke his heart, cried al a carte,
then hand wrote her a letter.
Feelings light as a feather,
Wishing we'll get back together.
But this P ain't for past,
more like progress, dumbass.
P don't even practice,
The boy shows up, and you bet he gets active.
P ain't got patience—time is now.
Although P can wait, never not present.
P ain't for pro, prep, or punk.
P never passed,
Flunk.
P flew miles for stamps,
His pages are cramped,
But P ain't for passport.
Dear Clinton Sparks, should I write more?
You see the P in her poise?

Found her pose on the wall,
It cost nothing to show ya'll,
But my property to write free and for all,
Selfish tendencies,
But who else can I call?
Poetically writing,
So let me stop,
…or I just stall.

¥

Bro, What?
March 7th, 2022

I'm a rover, dribbling across EARTH'S court of life,
Where a ball is my thoughts, weathering emotions.
The wind, my momentum, and calm is my timeout…
Stillness—next play—I draw out my thoughts.
Sometimes I'm down, and the ball is not falling,
And sometimes, through timeouts,
It's 'fuck you' to Spaulding…
Then I wipe this court clean,
Pristine as can see,
My sneakers go squeak,
Especially round' screens,
The basket…
Well, that's arbitrary,
But again, this ball,
It's weary—
You guessed it,
Shooting gets scary.
Free throws are bearing,
The opportunities are gusty,
Technical fouls for just staring,
Score points by a shoestring,
My teammate—a tree.
Wanna play me?
Just breathe.
…kidding,
Leave!
Byee,
¥

TikTokricy
March 14th, 2022

What's TikTok?

An analog clock?

Where your phone's the watch?

Awaiting dopamine shots,

From users who mock,

Perusers who caught,

Moments that shock,

Their nerves by the pop?

What if it's thought after thought?

Shared by those who are taught,

That phones are a prop,

Savoring lollis of pop,

So taste buds hop,

From a Tik,

To a Tok…

Am I off?

Or naw?

¥

WHEN I STARE AT THE MOON

Introduce Us
June 1st, 2022

I met me overseas,

It was me and only me,

But actually, it was three,

We're trilogies,

One old,

Call him 'G',

Retired free,

The other cold,

Don't call him at all,

Like autumn, he'll fall,

He's lanky—so tall,

Another short,

In fact, small,

So much,

He crawls,

He's the baby,

That's all,

He'll cry,

And that's all…

¥

WHEN I STARE AT THE MOON

Poise In Hair
June 3rd, 2022

You have permission to fight ignorance with itself,

Because it overpays,

And some are broke either way.

So regardless of truth and what they'll say,

Fighting fire with fire ignites the serpent's desire—

It's his playground,

Especially without GOD around.

While stacking ashes upon his sand mounds,

Evil on evil is fine, too—but they'll cut the grass,

And call them all snakes,

Pull her dreads as if they are fake.

One has never seen a locked head before,

Antennas detecting what's near to freeze, scorned.

…you can say that again.

And so, intelligence is poison,

It's how ignorance can pose a win.

¥

Baggage Dreams
June 10ᵗʰ, 2022

The best things in life come in threes,

Just like two bags when they're flying for free,

Plus one, the backpack I carry on and bring…

Aloof to the weight of each baggage's means,

…why care if they're holding the things that I need,

I'll cherish through flights and my childhood dreams,

Like where next should I take, and all of my things?

I'll wait til' it's easy,

Just wait here and breathe,

At home, I'll lounge,

And comfort my feet,

.

.

Zip, zip, it's the carbon encasement for me,

Wheels roll, it's the pulling and movement at ease,

When closed, it's the worlds en route I'll soon see,

…and now how my baggage,

Dreams onward with me,

Bye byeeee,

¥

WHEN I STARE AT THE MOON

Poetic Monster
July 25th, 2022

Through writings of BEAST, his word is sustained.
Humbled as he stumbled,
He stayed the fuck off Bumble,
So his inner world wouldn't crumble.
His money got right, and then his word grew ripe.
…awe, there are real monsters,
Who separates you from blessings.
When those close to you experience joy, recon that GOD
is next door,
Perusing his manifesto for your home's address, so…
Jealousy can be that monster,
shutting off porch lights.
From nights, he was curled on his concrete floor,
Crying, "Lord, Lord," guess who ignored?
From the mornings he awakened,
Asking, "Why, why?" Guess what he explored?
From the evenings, he prayed,
for not one but never a day,
There stood a body to implore.
Still standing at the gates of a—
"Fuck you," he walked away,
And light as a feather…
Untethered, fair-weathered, to see his true kiss.
From there lie enough stones,
From deprivation to build his throne.
He's not tired of being alone,
But fed up with the drones.
His duty, however, to protect the unknown,
First light, give a MOON,
Or a lovely red rose.

But only those of his father's garden,
For they shared a struggle,
As they forever grew pardoned,
But now, hardened.

¥

Poetic Flu
August 28th, 2022

I caught it drinking juice,

The Kool-Aids of my youth,

Coughing rounds of proof—

That I'm sick, with feelings of truth.

I caught it grabbing railings,

Above steps to higher sailings,

Looking down at past failings,

Blowing my nose, relieving the stuffings...

I got it from a rapper,

Mimicking rhyming rules,

Of memories so cruel,

Where gunshots ruled,

Yet also his survival tool.

I got it smelling a thief,

Who stole my adulting grief,

Now, no longer a boy,

But a man with awkward toys,

Thoughts of craving choice,

And grooming all six senses,

To define this fluetic sickness,

Cough, Cough,

Could it be contagious?

¥

WHEN I STARE AT THE MOON

Maverick
September 6th, 2022

Years of a creative athlete,
Now running out of Summer.
Years of a creative hustler,
Yet, he sucked.
But that time was needed to bust through…
And into the money-making man—
A Midnight bandit, robbing trains in trans,
Elusive to his band, and, he's nice.
He stole his ticket to the game,
Held up the store of hope…
Shaking down the banks of faith,
He never had to ask for it,
He knew it was his,
That's why he took it…
Creatively enough,
So that it's beautiful,
And those watching will see it as art,
…setting him spectrums apart.
He's the light that dark avoids,
He can't fix it, however…
A visual Band-aid,
And his athleticism,
It's the bandit in him…

¥

WHEN I STARE AT THE MOON

Watching Triggers
November 14th, 2022

You are with whom you star,

Rolling dice by triggering scars,

It's daunting, but here now's your part,

Sitting by death and its fool,

Who'll grab it—oh shit, that's their tool,

Click click, no more breaths, just a drool,

And screams by the blood drips, it pools,

Sounds harsh, but you brought this on you…

Don't run cause' that moment's in you,

To live by and learn about you,

And think next to triggering fools…

Who stand by their metal to duel.

¥

WHEN I STARE AT THE MOON

Fast Scar
February 18th, 2023

I wanna go fast,

Start me first or last,

Put me on the starting line,

Snatch the yoke, and I'll dash,

I'm gone & speeding to the cash,

So long …watch me drive, free alas,

Foot and I stab, pedal to the metal, I gas—

Break and dip like a cab …Or gas,

Break and skid to my pad,

Chill, I'm just a brag,

For real, speeding,

No drag, just a…

Poetic like,

Cringe—

…crash,

¥

WHEN I STARE AT THE MOON

Look Of Me
May 18th, 2024

Basking in your shadow,

Masking beams of light,

Dimming as you shade,

Your gleam….

It bends through night,

Recluse and so you hide,

. Elusive to your light,

Repulsed but—

You ain't shy…

Step out and let it lie,

Your aura, it glides,

Like starlight, it's bright,

Don't change when all is tied,

Don't say that you just tried,

Don't even when in binds,

But show up and let it die,

Old ways, old days,

Put on that branded cape,

Let fly—let drape,

The light and let them praise,

Those struggles from your grace,

Which carved your stony face,

Unveiled your noble fate,

And destined look of gaze,

¥

WHEN I STARE AT THE MOON

Project Batt
June 9th, 2024

How does it drive?
And why did I risk it?
Speeding til' gas,
Cost me a ticket,
I've paid it through patience,
By waiting,
And waiting,
…still love how I risk it,
Like white tees,
And brisket,
New turbos a twin,
Kin to my Mixons,
The paint…
Just mixey,
Shines blue,
But looks trippy,
The black tint,
It's risky,
And horses?
Just plenty,
400?
Add fifty,
You're kidding?
No—perching,
Like bat claws,
When dreaming
…or me off this Whiskey,

¥

WHEN I STARE AT THE MOON

Burn After Writing
July 8th, 2024

Is it hot in here, or is it just me?
Maybe it's me and the way I've gotta be.
Because I've gotta stay me in this skin containing me.
But ain't no containment since the artist in *eye,*
And *me,* whom you read,
Are making arrangements, you see?
Maybe it's the *BEAST* in me,
Painting the warriors of *eye?*
Or I who apologize because I cannot lie,
And I will not compromise until I die.
But even then, the *eye* of whom you read,
Will stay a bit longer to exhibit the heat of me,
Through the writings of *eye,* because…
That's the way it's gotta be—for me…
And I know it's selfish of me, but I own this of me,
And if I cannot be me, whose *eye* would I seek…?
Whose *me* would I try? Whose tear would I cry?
Because my tears don't lie nor dim my light.
They've run my skin from the hue of my kin.
Dripped through my feet, watering soils beneath.
…so here I write off the fires I've spoken,
Fires I dance and hilltops I've broke in,
Where upon each top, I ponder, and,
Muse into the paths, where today,
They remain carbon, soot filled,
And burned from the layers I've seared,

¥

Where Am From
July 25th, 2024

At the middle of my names,

Lies a road… it's paved by grace.

They drew no hash marks, no divide,

And through a Parish, where it hides.

Off these dirt roads, dusting pants,

Drivers pass, they wave—

…a smiling array,

.
.
.

I found the middle of my names,

Burning a SUN we lit, and MOON we hang…

Where bugs, who sang, could tune our name.

Each one intoned, mixed on a truce—

Where our dearly departed,

Can tell what's forgotten.

That this road, this land,

Ain't where we got started.

¥

WHEN I STARE AT THE MOON

For GOD To Move
November 2ⁿᵈ, 2024

What's good is GOD,

But we must've forgot,

How good it once got,

Like milk when it rots,

Or fish after caught—

As it sits and it flops,

Desperate for air,

Begging for water,

But remember…

When bothered,

Sit long and,

You'll falter,

…a matter,

Of faith—

Go move,

And feel,

Great,

¥

WHEN I STARE AT THE MOON

WHEN I STARE AT THE MOON (PART 3)

Today

…at first sight, its eyes were glowing. Its back hunched. And standing taller than my living room ceiling. Its arms bulged wider than my couch. Legs with more girth than my barstool table. Its stone-carved face presented just enough ease for me to gaze at its rocky, concrete-surfaced body. The figure stood modestly, lingering around the circumference of my tear-stained carpet. When it turned around to examine my wall, I saw that its back was a diamond-plated surface, where the top areas glistened and the corners dusted over.

With its back still to me, it shuffled its feet against the carpet stain, which startled me. Urine drizzled down my leg, and I immediately reached into the closet for a towel. But the figure abruptly jumped, turning to face my naked, panicking, frail body.

We stood in a contemplating stand-off, mimicking the zen energies of a master-to-student duo.

Then, it spread its arms wide, gathering both hands in a prayer-like pose. The figure then dropped to its knees, landing so violently in front of the stained area that its kneecaps crushed the concrete beneath my carpet. But as its eyes dimmed, it bowed its head, and we sat silently for nine musing breaths of mine.

On my tenth breath, the figure rubs the tips of its index and ring fingers until rocky debris is shed from its palms. It carefully spread the debris over the brown-stained area like a powdery substance or some type of carpet cleaner. The debris piled higher and higher, creating a three-foot-high mound of rocky dust over the stained area.

The figure stops. Brushes its palms off clean. And in admiration, watches dust run off the sides from the peak like powdered snow rushes down mountains during an avalanche. Once the mound is settled, its eyes lighten back up, and stands to its feet to inhale vigorously through its nostrils. Air is held in its expanded lungs long enough for me to re-wrap my towel around my waist because, all this time, I've been exposing some precious lumber.

But suddenly, the figure exhales forcefully through its mouth, blowing away the mound to where dust particles cover my walls, furniture, and stick to my dampened face and body.

Eventually, when the dust settled, the figure was gone.

(Continued on page 205)

¥

The Last MOON Of The Year
December 14ᵗʰ, 2018

You live in a world that'll grow you.

Don't ever expect it to owe you,

But to grow, you gotta want to.

Influencers…the people look up to you.

For your affluence, don't let either distort you,

Because the people have better views of you,

Their bird's eye views of you.

.
.

From the empty black sky above,

See again what lies in trust.

From below, like a telescope, only seeing what glows.

As the individual, though,

We're the Rockstar's from below.

Only seen because we humans glow.

Let the day go; this universe is for you to gloat.

.
.

Did you see the MOON last night?

I was born under it, and so was this rose,

And unknown to a few, I, too, was a bit soon.

'Twas Christmas Day, they say I was actually due.

.
.

Life—use it until it loses you.

If not, this likely won't amuse you.

Breathe well enough; it'll come very soon.

The holidays might be a reason for a gift to season.
Do it well; you'll be fortunate beyond reason.

.
.

Lastly, as the MOON last night showed,
We'll also see it go,
Like time was a foe, often soon to know,
Like some are doomed in snow,
Quite early, like my birthday, ya' know…?
Born 12-18, if you're curious to know,
It's never too late for that gift, slowpoke.
It'll come and go like our MOON, doe doe.

.
.

I was born at 12:18 AM,
Just after the last full MOON of 86' rose.
And so, like birth is to life, morning is to day.
Wanna know what our full MOONS won't say?
Is it odd it only shines during a full MOON stage?

¥

When A Star Reaches The Beach
March 2nd, 2019

While approaching the beach at night,
Each star above will teach our light that,
Crushed rocks are where the waters meet,
Rushing ashore as our feet soak, then sink.

.

I often look up at the night sky to view the stars,
To understand not much has changed,
Especially in the millions of years they've shined.
It amazes me how we see the same stars and,
Constellations people named thousands of years ago.

.

Whether it be science or history,
It won't matter if the most colorful one is Mars,
In that, some of the lights we see up there,
They died several millenniums ago.
Yet today, a star is as bright as our dead generations,
And the ones in clusters, like church congregations.

.

The moment you hit the sand,
The taste of vacation is felt on command.
Walking into oceans,
Feeling cooler than the salts in motion.
The rush of ocean water is inviting,
Because the SUN, heat, and sweat,
...are what you could be fighting.

.

.

Reaching the beach where the stars gleam to teach;
a fiery abundance is what the SUN will repeat.
Looking anywhere near it is painfully dumb,
Like looking at a star is boring but only—
...for those that are far from one.

.

.

As night skies remind us, we aren't the brightest,
These stars don't shine on each other but unite us.
When they do, it's a glaring space to combine us...

.

.

SUNLIGHT at the equator may hit different, so be it,
aiding our star of EARTH to shine better as heat is;
...reflecting light for others viewing from afar,
To think, wow, what a beautiful shining hue of a star.

.

.

A fool doesn't look at the SUN for fun.
A fool will likely compare,
...explaining the fire it shuns.
Stars don't shine on each other in view,
And as a night on the beach will make,
An intergalactic but humbling stage,
Each star as it sits, resting its phase,
Watching you gaze,
Without calling its name,

¥

An Awakening Of One Million Creators
October 9ᵗʰ, 2019

If 3:00 AM should wake me up,
Here's how it would sound.
Knocking from door to door,
a mere shift through town.
We'd make it, until now, fake it,
Because our faith's never taken.
Time is key.
You've done the rare,
In the mind because most wouldn't see you there.
Spinning be your foe at the end of the tunnel.
Blinking in disbelief, looking back at fumbles.
You're meant to succeed,
It's why, through the fork, you proceed.
Traveled a road less chosen,
Challenging fate, easily broken.
Facing past failures, re-stamp the passport,
and enter with cohorts.
We woke you for the unbroke you.
To become the success you see in proof,
We need you, we requested you,
…our people are waiting for you.

¥

WHEN I STARE AT THE MOON

A Message From Behind The Stars
December 15th, 2019

What is this place?
Where the flute sends its touch from a retro wave.
Questions delay a process as sounds create the space.
Atop still waters, can we unite?
Pondering there as warm air travels between argon.
The hurt was yesteryear, the suffering is still;
But a guardian eagle soars above in peace.
So calm—as the other four moods await their turn. Care
to explain such a state?
A walk through water.
Swimming in the fire.
Climbing the gases of ether.
Take a bow, for you did not explain—
But rather, the hills of this land express you.
Fear was the propeller.
Right eyes, right time.
Because we are enough.
We are just… beauty.
It becomes relative down there.
Here it is, everywhere and forever.
Pain, obliviated.
Don't talk about it; we might go back.
When the lad asks for help, revisit in context.
They need to know where you truly were at.
Because few believe.
But enough will always.
And that doesn't go anywhere.
However, you do—

¥

WHEN I STARE AT THE MOON

Stargazing For Whom I Look Up To
January 18th, 2020

Above shining and beneath your surface,
a burning crust.
Dirty minds rhyme with what creates us,
It's between us men.
A divided line of trials.
Eleven miles, and for each a breath, I smile.
You all are respected in gratitude.
I created a beautiful mess; now, here I elude.
Of the childish nature in *eye*, the deed is shy.
Every moment walking into my why.
A runner's bliss—why am I here?
Because the idea defends a cry.
My words are nothing to you.
But fate's virtue; so, who is *eye*?
A writing bird, protecting verbs.
In other words, I'm here to write.
Take action on my fights.
And you I look up to,
A hero tonight.
Running next to stars,
Wishing upon the hottest.
Bold next to the modest.
A planet I see is the brightest.
I run with you in view.
Like Venus,
I could be running for you.

¥

Our Words Are Here, But Where's Our Head?
January 19th, 2020

And then we keep going up in time—
there's no turning back.
Where's this Monday going with our lives?
When's this dream ending this scene?
As life's a mother-fucker,
it continues to birth you sons of bitches.
There will come a time when the creative wild-child will
write a book in your country.
Words had to make home first.
The dog stares a lot—what's the move, human?
For this Monday mood, think love and never, rude.
Don't wish it were a Friday;
These days, they just repeat themselves—
…they promise.
If you have a battle going on,
Write it on paper and then spit on it.
It's all a blur now.
If thoughts were as light as my bird's feather,
why does paper carry such merit?
We must think before writing,
like a bird must hear before speaking,
Or, a boxer trains before fighting.
But does the SUN practice before shining?
We'd been died, you see…
We're a happening of love inviting.
Thoughts creating Mondays…
that your dreams are trying.
How random are our differences?
We think, but have separate instances…

¥

A Journey Which Doesn't Know How, Can Only....
March 4ᵗʰ, 2020

There, it rose above the horizon.
They stare, and thunder roars uprising.
Their eyes to share as rainfall surprises them.
The cattle chew bare, and grass proceeds them.
Goodnight, and from there, a morning kiss returns.
Our distant love so young as time we miss.
Where art thou faith to take it today?
Into a stirring of things by those unseen.
Laughter up yonder is now serene.
A hand to grab, I made it by dream.
Night in, night out, emotions to fight.
Dwelling within to win and unite.
Envisions of how we all take flight.
A game to watch as many breathe in.
No shame to carry, my brothers of kin.
Hearing true stories, as each will tell it…
From podiums of truth, some will yell it.
First, we failed them at winning again.
Second, will be a feast of jive chickens.
Third is a world of verbs to elate.
May the fourth be waters of eternal great lakes.
With you, my words will often create—
Happiness; I am real and never a fake.
But faith has taken all of my ways.
Unable to prove, somehow I grew.
Just watch me, today,
I often don't know…
Journeying as if, I only know so—
¥

WHEN I STARE AT THE MOON

If We Read Art In Its Colored Context
May 26th, 2020

I promise you'll have enough dreams to choose from.
After every morning, reach the awesome feeling so you
won't lose one.
It'll be in your karma to repurpose the ugly ones.
We're ordinary people dreaming of an alternative life to
veer from.
Act as you know, though you don't, so your imagination
flows on.
Count to three, take a breath, and drive through the
illusions of stress.
And face fear; for the other side,
dreams come undone.
It's scary, like a negro named Larry, but...
He'll be the one pissing his pants as courage outweighs
weary, thus...
Forever going forth each fork in the road; dare me.
Anxieties of my past which got me here;
bear with me.
Stories of the fool who dreams daily without rules...
How embarrassing?
A journey so rare, but unto you I pray to share;
Join for free.
Stillness through the night and breathing mighty light;
births new life.
Thinking overnight allows visions to show what's right,
but there is a price.
A becoming of the black sheep; an insane repeat...
Of good things no one sees,
And managing our negative peeps'.
For those who see, them who see when shown,

And they who choose not to see,
...for I've repeated Leonardo Da Vinci.
An appreciation to a passing artist and a feature photo
into this poetic read.
This concludes today's memorial of an artist sharing an
alternative humane dream.
And a reminder of how our colors misrepresent,
Not most, but a whole lot of things.

¥

Write Your Stand For The Star Of Life
June 9ᵗʰ, 2020

Bold—as they configure who you are.
No longer stalking each star,
But eager to pass par.
We beneath this skin are not vulnerable.
But with strong stones for our history's noble.
For what is white, the dark distinguishes in art.
For what's black, the light replenishes apart.
For what's grey, we place in the middle to start.
It's where we are because stories are often a la carte.
Depends on how you wanna' tell it if you're picking our
colors apart.
Like a star, and how they'd name it to sound smart.
We breathe the same air; we see the same light…
So why are we seeing a different fight?
As each star shines out the same dark…
We walk a path to put another behind bars.
We talk a sound to hear an alien sound from afar.
Later, exile those who simply embark.
Til' Babylon falls, and a baby learns to crawl…
Let's learn the four types of US:
Those who follow orders, lead orders,
and those who question orders.
For those who watch orders,
Hold futures within like borders.
They are thought hoarders.
Emerging as stars who infiltrate the followers.
Correcting leaders who ignore true philosophers.
And connecting the questioners,
Who'll weave lost dwellers.
We are one tribe, tangled by vibes,
and with colorful strides…
We prevail.
We are the star of life.
¥

WHEN I STARE AT THE MOON

You Ought To Be A Star Among Rocks
July 21st, 2020

I am a rock.
The waves come, and wind knocks.
I smile.
Welcome to your home for a while.
It's a beach, so beware of sand,
It's the tricky part of this land.
You could sink, fall and be damned.
But since we're like water, you'll flow,
As does water upon its waves' approach.
You're a rock.
No one sees the connection.
Like sand, we're close.
More than most.
Water rushes.
Washes our surface.
Crashed into by oceans.
Creating rivers in motion.
For views bringing a smile.
From how far?
The bliss in between each mile…
At the next star, you see.
Be a rock as you are.
Floating in peace,
Smile.
We're a rock, you see.
Look up.
…it's you from afar.
Glowing like a rockstar

¥

WHEN I STARE AT THE MOON

Moon, You Full As Fuck Right Now
August 23rd, 2021

Tonight, you've got a brightened face, glowing.
Last night, you hid that face, behind clouds; why so?
I don't know, but I cannot sleep.
And so, at this hour, what must I think?
Waiting for my next book's proof copy delivery—
Which represents me writing through hell.
As if the world cared about their—
Moon child,
Moon writer,
Writing fighter,
Midnights by her,
Suicide survivor,
Dreams encouraged her.
Stood on my feet beside her.
The water was rocky.
New leg muscles to prop me.
Then, she left me.
Heart thief!
But am not sad, you see…
Some are protected, like me, from heat.
Not of a light, but an effortless hype.
Moon writing through night.
Soon flying—how nice?
I'm done here.
Goodnight.
¥

WHEN I STARE AT THE MOON

Hello MOON

September 20th, 2021

Out of darkness, you rise.
#AmWriting but not surprised…
You're full for now.
I'll call you about…
The means I need and now.
For sure and no doubt,
You'll provide in time profound.
You told me this.
Be happy, be still,
I am all I want.
Do not flaunt.
Many in contrast, taunt.
It's how they're taught.
A MOON without—a MOON with all.
Same MOON, new breath.
A reminder to never stress.
A kiss.
Soon, by her, I'll caress.
And feel her dress.
Her eyes that're blessed.
Keep it PG.
A MOON so bright,
…same bulb of light,
Up high to unite us.
Down low, how does it find us?
In peace by a MOON.
EARTH Angel,
…see you soon.

¥

New MOON, Who dis?
February 3rd, 2022

At the end of my final run through Cairo, per usual, I sprinted the last 100 yards. After slowing down, I ran back-paddling for about 20 yards, facing ongoing traffic. I then blew kisses at a couple drivers and took two bows as I placed my arms behind and in front of me. When I turned around to stop, I gave thanks to the higher powers above, and proceeded to ask myself, "Who the fuck do you think you are?"

Before that moment, I was the world's greatest runner—because I'm undefeated against my opponents.

I never ran in high school—in fact, I've never competed against anyone, in general. My competition is me.

With each run, I get better. It's hard to explain if you've never physically challenged yourself.

Why I blew kisses and bowed at those cars is irrelevant. I'm more concerned with the question I asked myself. I mean, can I be great? Damn…

Since I've thought about it, the kisses were for me, and the bows were for my running self. Think of it like this— no one's thanking me for running my heart out but me. And no one's benefiting from these runs but me. Selfish or not, I'm a millennial bachelor who thinks all the aliens are hiding at airports.

Me doing something out of the ordinary is just that.

New MOON, who dis'?

Okay?

Bye.

¥

WHEN I STARE AT THE MOON

One Eye Love

March 15ᵗʰ, 2022

Of all the lights in our universe, I chose you. You illuminate, dim, and then you suddenly brighten. From there, I must cover my eyes.

I can feel that your colors only matter when the mood is important. Once in a while, you're blue, and when our SUN goes down, you're yellow. Mixing the two makes you green. So, are you where the money is? Although eyes do brighten when money is in sight, I wouldn't think so.

Is it true that your light is my reflection?

It sure answers the question of why space is dark— because if the SUN is so bright, then why is it black out there?

The short answer is that light needs a canvas. It needs dust. It needs us, who need water. EARTH'S atmosphere has the perfect chemical exchange—where we are the source by which light reflects.

And there are well over eight billion of us. So again, I chose you. Shall we make this a novel exchange?

Love has no color.

¥

WHEN I STARE AT THE MOON

Low Fidelity
March 19th, 2022

If you lose your one and only,
There's a MOON as bright to soul seek.
It's cold, but don't be so scared now; walk free.
Hold back, but boldly, those tears don't show me.
I've wasted enough on weak sheep, dumb me,
But sheer we are shameless and growing,
Here, we're scared—don't blame me,
I try, I tried, some warned me,
I'm done, ok, surrendering,
You win, I hurt,
Byeee…

¥

Star Bathing
November 6th, 2022

We know who you are,
But we won't stare,
…you don't blink, do you?
Your light, your halo,
Glistens at your step,
Molding an amazing depth,
So light, we feel at ease,
Like a feather, your aura's a breeze,
We'll head to our vehicle,
But first, grab keys,
We'd like to follow,
At least your shadow,
If lucky,
Bask through your halo,
¥

WHEN I STARE AT THE MOON

An Astronaut's Pick

December 26th, 2022

Opulent in growth,
A visual oath,
Steer us,
Prepare them,
But do not dare,
Fear the path to each,
That is, an uphill journey,
Against the wind, into abyss,
Until we're floating in bliss,
Looking back like, oh shit,
We're here, so don't trip,
It's fun as you flip,
Turning to kick,
Head dipping,
Just kick,
Falling?
Kick,

¥

WHEN I STARE AT THE MOON

Some Of The Moon

June 27ᵗʰ, 2024

Sum of time's past,
By a summons of my path,
Did some of those wrong,
For a sum and still broke,
Feeling stuck, counting dimes,
Wheeling where they wine and dine,
Wasn't driving—but I thrived,
Dropping bags of goods through night,
Passing bars until goodnight,
…watching MOONS up high so bright,
I walked the SUN—I walked to fight,
And ran til' numb—yes…all night,

¥

WHEN I STARE AT THE MOON

Stars Under The Lids

November 24th, 2024

Whosoever's dark place I've entered,
Don't be so kind—I am no guest,
I shed a light, and despite…
Your patterning protest.
Don't scorn me a parasite,
Because I promise to walk on by—
Yet, parade up high between dust and,
Star mites…Probing down below,
I've seen you come to avoid,
This space, or like a void,
You left empty, and,
…annoyed

¥

WHEN I STARE AT THE MOON

When I Stare At The Moon (Part 4)
Tomorrow

…that wasn't very nice, now was it?

But there I stood. My sofa lathered in a fine coat of dust. My coffee table smothered in crushed sulfur. And my kitchen countertops, television, and walls resembling the Greater Northwest after the 1981 Mount St. Helens eruption. The rocky grey figure left nothing behind but my living room looking like a dark, pearly white brushed chalkboard.

I swiped a layer of dust off the coffee table and rubbed it between my fingers, questioning, "Was the figure even here?" I patted the carpet, checking the padding beneath for crushed concrete, but it was solid without any cracks. No footprints were on my dusty carpet, either—but the dust on my hands and face was all that felt real.

Maybe the figure was all but my imagination—because even my body felt light enough to wonder if my run up 13th Avenue was also my imagination. Shouldn't my quads feel sore? And my hamstrings be tender? Or my calves feel tight?

Come to think of it, why was I even running?

I burst into laughter because that's what silly people do when confused. Eventually, I laughed until my eyes shed enough tears to wash dust down my dirty cheeks, leaving tear tracks down my dusty, lonesome face. I continued laughing so hard that my knees weakened and my abs cramped—causing me to drop to the floor and lie on my back against the dusty carpet. The last I remember was extending my legs and arms to move them against the dusty carpet as if I were engraving a snow angel.

.

.

It's been sixteen years since I encountered the stone-faced figure on my living room carpet. Even though its face has faded from my memory, when I stare at the MOON, its face emerges across the surface—resembling its stoic expression—hanging in the dark Willamette Black canvasing skies of Poetland.

Which can get pretty awkward when running beneath a full MOON as I feel its eyes piercing my sclera whites. It also reminds me of how I felt that day when my soul was emptied, and my breaths were carried across my palms as if I'd awakened from a sweat-induced nightmare.

¥

Spaceships On Poetland

December 15th, 2024

Weird things come and go, but those who see them stay around forever to chant about it well past their transition. It's a phenomenal conception of the unapologetic asshole who set their cities on fire and paint over the soot with the blood of dummies.

These are not martyrs or murderers. But their suits include a hoodie that's the same color as the walls of my neurotic red room. They sell a fragrance reminding me of the day I spoke to the nail protruding from my college apartment's bedroom door frame—who kept whispering, "You don't belong here…"

They gave their leader such a name that commands full use of the human tongue. But I learned how to utter it during a dream I had, where I performed sonnets for The Children of the Sphere.

The more I think about them, the more I think I'm copying and pasting the essence of their predicament—where they claim to have stolen a mile from our skies to get here. Which was hard to believe until I gazed long enough over the skyline of Portland and saw the writings of their MOONS.

¥

I Read Your Moon

January 2nd, 2025

Is it because I'm new?
Hanging high and no eyes for you?
Take a picture; yes, I'm such a beautiful view.
But naturally so, I only move when amused,
Like your assumptions of color,
As if my brother shines yellow,
Or blanket's dark blue…
In space, they're a plight,
Hung by the eyes,
Of our scholarly scribes;
Did you read them, alright?
Or is the white all too bright?
If so, we're not sorry,
Our pen ink is teary,
It's shed out the eyes,
By the kids of our weary,

¥

WHEN I STARE AT THE MOON

In Root

February 23rd, 2025

Where the bottom is water,
We fish,
Then falter.
Where swimming,
Gets awkward,
Like Anglers,
Or Gulpers…
It's ugly,
Til' next,
Where midpoint,
We float,
We coast,
Then probe,
And wait til' we're told;
Go takeoff,
Go lift-off,
En route to,
Our root cause,

¥